Excavating the Power of Memory in Japan

Excavating the power of memory offers a succinct examination of how memory is constructed, embedded and disseminated in contemporary Japanese society. The unique range and perspective of this collection will provide an understanding not found elsewhere. It starts with a lucid introduction of how memory plays a political and wider social role in Japan. Four case studies follow. The first takes up the divergence in memory at the national and subnational levels by analysing the memory of the battle of Okinawa and US military accidents in Okinawa prefecture, illuminating how memory in the prefecture embeds Okinawans as victims of mainland Japan and of the United States. The second explores whether Japan's membership of the International Criminal Court represents a shift in the Japanese government's negative remembrance of the International Military Tribunal for the Far East, demonstrating how both courts are largely portrayed as being disconnected in political debates. The third interrogates and compares the presumed identity of the members of the Kamikaze Special Attack Unit in the dominant collective memory and their own self-identities, offering insights from an in-depth discourse study of the Kamikazes' surviving letters through integrated qualitative and quantitative analyses of the largest digitised database to date. The fourth untangles how the 'memory of winds' in Japanese fishing communities remains an expression of social thought that presides over the 'transmission of meaning' about fishermen's geographical surroundings.

This book was previously published as a special issue of the *Japan Forum*.

Glenn D. Hook is Toshiba International Foundation Anniversary Research Professor in the School of East Asian Studies, University of Sheffield, UK. His recent publications include *Regional Risk and Security in Japan: Whither the Everyday* (co-author, Routledge, 2015) and *Japan's International Relations: Politics, Economics and Security*, third edition, (co-author, Routledge, 2012).

Excavating the Power of Memory in Japan

Edited by
Glenn D. Hook

LONDON AND NEW YORK

First published 2016
by Routledge
2 Park Square, Milton Park, Abingdon, Oxon, OX14 4RN, UK

and by Routledge
711 Third Avenue, New York, NY 10017, USA

Routledge is an imprint of the Taylor & Francis Group, an informa business

Chapters 1, 3–5 © 2016 British Association for Japanese Studies
Chapter 2 © Glenn D. Hook

All rights reserved. No part of this book may be reprinted or reproduced or utilised in any form or by any electronic, mechanical, or other means, now known or hereafter invented, including photocopying and recording, or in any information storage or retrieval system, without permission in writing from the publishers.

Trademark notice: Product or corporate names may be trademarks or registered trademarks, and are used only for identification and explanation without intent to infringe.

British Library Cataloguing in Publication Data
A catalogue record for this book is available from the British Library

ISBN 13: 978-1-138-67729-6

Typeset in Plantin
by RefineCatch Limited, Bungay, Suffolk

Publisher's Note
The publisher accepts responsibility for any inconsistencies that may have arisen during the conversion of this book from journal articles to book chapters, namely the possible inclusion of journal terminology.

Disclaimer
Every effort has been made to contact copyright holders for their permission to reprint material in this book. The publishers would be grateful to hear from any copyright holder who is not here acknowledged and will undertake to rectify any errors or omissions in future editions of this book.

Contents

Citation Information	vii
Notes on Contributors	ix
1. Excavating the power of memory in Japan *Glenn D. Hook*	1
2. The American eagle in Okinawa: the politics of contested memory and the unfinished war *Glenn D. Hook*	4
3. From Tokyo to The Hague: war crime tribunals and (shifting?) memory politics in Japan *Kerstin Lukner*	26
4. Contested memories of the Kamikaze and the self-representations of Tokkō-tai youth in their missives home *Luli van der Does-Ishikawa*	50
5. Invisible landscapes. Winds, experience and memory in Japanese coastal fishery *Giovanni Bulian*	85
Index	111

Citation Information

The chapters in this book were originally published in *Japan Forum*, volume 27, issue 3 (September 2015). When citing this material, please use the original page numbering for each article, as follows:

Chapter 1
Excavating the power of memory in Japan
Glenn D. Hook
Japan Forum, volume 27, issue 3 (September 2015), pp. 295–298

Chapter 2
The American eagle in Okinawa: the politics of contested memory and the unfinished war
Glenn D. Hook
Japan Forum, volume 27, issue 3 (September 2015), pp. 299–320

Chapter 3
From Tokyo to The Hague: war crime tribunals and (shifting?) memory politics in Japan
Kerstin Lukner
Japan Forum, volume 27, issue 3 (September 2015), pp. 321–344

Chapter 4
Contested memories of the Kamikaze and the self-representations of Tokkō-tai youth in their missives home
Luli van der Does-Ishikawa
Japan Forum, volume 27, issue 3 (September 2015), pp. 345–379

Chapter 5
Invisible landscapes. Winds, experience and memory in Japanese coastal fishery
Giovanni Bulian
Japan Forum, volume 27, issue 3 (September 2015), pp. 380–404

For any permission-related enquiries please visit:
http://www.tandfonline.com/page/help/permissions

Notes on Contributors

Giovanni Bulian, PhD, is Adjunct Lecturer in the Department of Asian and North African Studies, Ca' Foscari University of Venice, Italy. His research interests include environmental anthropology, small-scale fisheries and anthropology of climate.

Glenn D. Hook is Toshiba International Foundation Anniversary Research Professor in the School of East Asian Studies, University of Sheffield, UK. His recent publications include *Regional Risk and Security in Japan: Whither the Everyday* (co-author, Routledge, 2015) and *Japan's International Relations: Politics, Economics and Security*, third edition, (co-author, Routledge, 2012).

Kerstin Lukner is a Post-Doctoral Research Fellow at the Institute of East Asian Studies, University of Duisburg-Essen, Germany, and academic coordinator of the Alliance for Research on East Asia (AREA Ruhr). Her research has been published widely and focuses on Japan in multilateral organizations, Japanese security policy and Asia's dealing with trans-boundary health risks.

Luli van der Does-Ishikawa (MSc, MPhil, PhD) is a Visiting Scholar of the research team, 'War Crimes and Empire', Faculty of Asian and Middle Eastern Studies, University of Cambridge, UK. She specializes in the interdisciplinary quantitative and qualitative study of Japanese language, people and society. Her recent research has focused on the process of ideological transfer through discursive communication in media and the shifting loci of risk and responsibility.

Excavating the power of memory in Japan

GLENN D. HOOK

This special issue on excavating the power of memory in Japan explores how memory is contested in a number of divergent fields of research. Its temporal focus is on narrating the past and memory from the 1940s, including memory of the war then and in the post-war era. Much of the extant work in Japanese Studies has focused on the memory of the war and how this memory is contested across the boundaries of the state as well as domestically. Internationally, a particular area of concern has been the different interpretations, narratives and memory of the war in Japan compared with China and South Korea, as in disputes over the 'rape of Nanking' and the 'comfort women' (Yoshida 2006, Soh 2009). Another area of concern has been the comparison of the Japanese and German cases and their different approaches to the past (Berger 2012). Other, more recent, work has taken up the changing role of museums in commemorating the past in Japan, China and South Korea (Yoshida 2014). Domestically, work on the high degree of contestation over how history is interpreted and remembered highlights a lively debate over the Japanese past, not simply 'amnesia' (Seaton 2010). The point is reinforced by recent work detailing the role of civic groups in contesting the memory of the Asia- Pacific war at the grassroots level (Szczepanska 2014).

As seen most recently when Prime Minister Abe Shinzō went to Yasukuni shrine in December 2013, the differing interpretations, narrations and memories of the war are not locked away in an ivory tower, but rather exert a profound impact on the diplomatic relations between Japan and its two most important neighbours, China and South Korea. The lack of summits between Abe and the Chinese and Korean leaders are a clear indication of the diplomatic nadir affecting regional relations in the wake of the prime minister's visit to the shrine. Whether Abe's action represents a revival of Japanese militarism, on the road to Japan becoming the Harry Potter villain, Lord Voldemort, as charged by the Chinese ambassador to the UK (*Daily Telegraph* 1 January 2014), or rather represents the prime minister praying for peace, as his Japanese counterpart claimed a few days later (*Daily Telegraph* 5 January 2014), divides the two ambassadors as it does many in both countries. What is clear, however, is how the role of the shrine in interring the souls of fourteen convicted A-class war criminals and in hosting the Yūshūkan museum, which glorifies the war, means any visit to Yasukuni by the prime minister of Japan will remain politically charged. Clearly, memory and commemoration of the war has contemporary as well as historical significance at both government and popular levels.

Research on memory underscores how divergent memories coexist and are contested in Japan, not only as seen above in terms of the international and domestic differences over the Asia-Pacific war, but also in terms of daily practices in different communities. Three of the articles making up this special issue focus on different aspects of the memory of the war, whilst the fourth broadens our perspective on how memory is contested in Japan by focusing on the case of local fishing communities, where the memory of daily practices informs daily life. What unites the four articles making up this special issue is their focus on how memory is contested and deployed by different actors, whether those promoting divergent memories at the national and subnational levels; individual memory of the war and how the memory has been exploited politically in the postwar years; the legal implications of how the war is remembered; and how memory is put to use in daily life by fishermen.

The first article by Glenn Hook investigates the divergence between national and subnational memory in Japan by examining how the memories of the Battle of Okinawa and key US military accidents in the Occupation and post-Occupation eras are linked in a way to oppose the unequal concentration of American bases in Okinawa. Hook argues that the politics of contested memory in the prefecture constructs, embeds and disseminates a memory of Okinawans as victims of the national government in Tokyo as well as of the United States. This dual victimization is at the heart of the ongoing struggle against the 'unfinished war' in the prefecture. The next article by Kerstin Lukner explores whether Japan's membership of the International Criminal Court (ICC) hints at a partial shift in its critical assessment and negative remembrance of the International Military Tribunal for the Far East (IMTFE). Her analysis shows that both courts are largely portrayed as being disconnected in political debates as decision-makers either highlight the legal improvements of the ICC when compared with the 'flawed' IMTFE or ignore their evolutionary lineage altogether. For Japan, the accession to the ICC was primarily a chance to stress its post-war identity as a law-abiding member of the international community, reconfiguring the contested IMTFE-induced image of the country as an aggressive pariah. Luli van der Does-Ishikawa then moves the discussion on to a quantitative and qualitative exploration of the first-hand experience recorded in the surviving letters that the Kamikaze pilots wrote. The Kamikazes' presumed identities and psychology attributed in dominant collective memory contrast sharply with the Kamikazes' self-identities in their mental landscape as narrated by themselves. Belligerence against humanity was nearly absent in the missives. Instead, description of emotional turmoil and a youthful search for (self-) identity predominate. In the post-war era, ever-diversifying images of the Kamikazes ensued due to the missives being narrated from the second- and third-person perspectives. The final article, by Giovani Bulian, untangles how the 'memory of winds' in Japanese fishing communities is still an expression of social thought that presides over the 'transmission of meaning' about fishermen's geographical surroundings. His article demonstrates how Japanese fishermen's memory is implicitly subversive of the dominant discourses on ecological knowledge in Japan, generally focused on its *epistemological* hierarchization (folk and scientific knowledge), or on the individualization of the cultural discrepancies between traditional and contemporary knowledge.

Acknowledgements

This Special Issue is a result of research conducted under the umbrella of the National Institute of Japanese Studies, part of the White Rose East Asia Centre (http://www.wreac.org/), a centre of excellence between the universities of Sheffield and Leeds. The articles were first presented at a workshop of East Asia Net (http://www.eastasianet.eu/) held at the University of Sheffield in April 2014 and the revised versions were then presented at a June workshop in Sheffield. We are grateful to the Arts and Humanities Research Council for the funding of these events.

The authors also wish to thank the anonymous reviewers for their comments and the *Japan Forum* editorial team for their support.

References

Berger, T., 2012. *War, guilt and world politics after world war II*. Cambridge: Cambridge University Press.
Seaton, P.A., 2010. *Japan's contested war memories: the 'memory rifts' in historical consciousness of world war II*. London: Routledge.
Soh, C.S., 2009. *The comfort women: sexual violence and postcolonial memory in Korea and Japan*. Chicago: University of Chicago Press.
Szczepanska, K., 2014. *The politics of memory in Japan. Progressive civil society groups and contestation of memory of the Asia-Pacific war*. London: Routledge.
Yoshida, T. 2006. *The making of the 'rape of Nanking': history and memory in Japan, China and the United States*. New York: Oxford University Press.
Yoshida, T., 2014. *From cultures of war to cultures of peace: war and peace museums in Japan, China and South Korea*. Portland, Maine: MerwinAsia.

The American eagle in Okinawa: the politics of contested memory and the unfinished war

GLENN D. HOOK

Abstract: This article on contested memory and the 'unfinished war' in Okinawa explores the link between the memories of the battle of Okinawa and US military accidents in the prefecture, on the one hand, and the calls to reduce US installations, on the other. National government policy-makers and security managers view Okinawa's outposts of American power as an essential ingredient in a security policy aimed at deterring potential enemies, whether these are identified as the Soviet Union during the Cold War, or a rising China and a nuclear-armed North Korea today. But the unequal distribution and concentration of US bases in the prefecture and the military accidents associated with their operation mean the memories of the battle of Okinawa and of US military accidents have become a political resource for opponents of the bases. The article demonstrates how these memories serve to embed Okinawans as victims of the national government as well as of the United States, manifest as a contestation between collective memory at the national and prefectural levels.

1. Introduction

This article excavates the power of memory by investigating how the politics of contested memory and the 'unfinished war' in Okinawa interrogates the link between the memories of the Battle of Okinawa and US military accidents in the prefecture, on the one hand, and the calls to reduce the presence of US installations, on the other.[1] National government policy-makers and security managers view US military facilities in the prefecture as integral to the US–Japan alliance and as an essential ingredient in the security of Japan. From their perspective, these outposts of the American eagle play a vital role in the deterrence of potential adversaries, whether these are identified as the Soviet Union during the Cold War, or a rising China and a nuclear-armed North Korea today. In other words,

© 2015 The Authors. Published by Taylor & Francis.
This is an Open Access article distributed under the terms of the Creative Commons Attribution License (http://creativecommons.org/Licenses/by/4.0/), which permits unrestricted use, distribution, and reproduction in any medium, provided the original work is properly cited.

American military forces in Okinawa are viewed as offering security against Japan becoming the victim of an external aggressor, suggesting how their role is seen as contributing to a collective good for the benefit of all in Japan (on security as a collective good, see Rothschild 1995, pp. 63–64).

However, US bases in Japan, purportedly for the benefit of all, pose a risk to the everyday security of Okinawans (Hook *et al.* 2015). This is particularly the case as American forces are unequally distributed amongst Japanese prefectures and are concentrated overwhelmingly in the Okinawa prefecture, which hosts nearly three-quarters of the military installations used solely by the American military (for details, see Okinawa Prefectural Government 2013). Due to the resistance of other prefectures to hosting US bases, maintaining this unequal distribution in US deployments remains an overriding goal of policy-makers and security managers on both sides of the Pacific. Indeed, the present Abe Shinzō administration has been devoting considerable energy to perpetuating this inequality by seeking to gain the prefecture's acquiescence in the relocation of Marine Corps Air Station Futenma from the heavily populated city of Ginowan to the sparsely populated Henoko district of Nago city, including the construction of part of the new facilities off-shore Henoko in the environmentally fragile Oura Bay (*Okinawa Taimuzu*, 7 August 2014; McCormack and Oka Norimatsu 2012).

True, the prefectural population supports the 1996 Special Action Committee on Okinawa's (SACO) agreement between the US and Japanese governments to reduce the burden of the bases on Okinawa (Ministry of Foreign Affairs 1996). More than that, though, nearly three-quarters favour the relocation of the base outside of the prefecture or outside of Japan and remain steadfastly opposed to moving Futenma within the prefecture. In a poll conducted in May 2014, for instance, 74 per cent of the pollees expressed opposition to the relocation of the Futenma air station to another part of Okinawa (*Ryūkyū Shimpō*, 15 May 2014). At the political level, too, a survey of the forty-five members of the prefectural assembly found a majority of twenty-six, 58 per cent, unwilling to support the transfer of the Futenma air station to Henoko (*Ryūkyū Shimpō*, 13 August 2014). Another survey of the mayors and other political leaders of the cities, towns and villages in the prefecture found 53 per cent opposed to the relocation (*Okinawa Taimuzu*, 9 June 2014). Clearly, the continued presence of the Futenma base in Okinawa, whether in Ginowan or relocated to Henoko, symbolizes the unwillingness of the government to tackle the underlying problem of the unequal concentration of US bases in the prefecture, even if the everyday security of a much smaller percentage of the prefectural population would be at risk from the new base due to the lower number of residents in Henoko compared with Ginowan.

One of the perennial concerns of the people of Okinawa is how the existence and operations of US military installations have led to a range of incidents, such as robbery and rape, as well as accidents, such as aircraft crashes and mishaps. The potential for aircraft accidents in the prefecture continues to pose a risk to the local population, especially those living in close proximity to the Kadena Air Base and Futenma. Indeed, the memory of earlier military crashes and mishaps involving aircraft from these two bases reinforces the sense of everyday risk faced by the local population as a consequence of US military deployments in the prefecture. Whilst the most serious air crashes occurred during the twenty-seven years of American Occupation of Okinawa from 1945 until 1972, the Occupation's end did not bring to an end aircraft accidents, per se (Okinawa Prefectural Government 2013a, p. 104). This means that, instead of viewing the American military forces as a deterrent and as a protector of Japan from potential external aggressors, as with national policy-makers and security managers, many residents in Okinawa instead view these foreign forces as a risk to their own everyday life and security, as at the time of the Battle of Okinawa in 1945.

As we will examine in detail below, this representation of Okinawans as dual victims – of incidents and accidents caused by American military deployments as well as of the unequal distribution of the bases as a result of the national government's security policy – is linked to the memory of a similar dual victimization of Okinawans by Americans and mainland Japanese during the Battle of Okinawa. The cost to Okinawa was a large loss of civilian life, not only due to the American invasion of the islands but also to the activities of imperial troops. The survivors of the *himeyuri* nursing corps who act as *kataribe* (narrators) at the Himeyuri Peace Museum and elsewhere tell of how, as nurses, they were victimized by both American and Japanese soldiers (Himeyuri n.d.; Miyagi 1995). This historical link between the land battle and the continued US military presence in and victimization of Okinawa epitomizes the unfinished war for the people of the prefecture. In an era when the American eagle has become emblematic of the local environment and military installations are but one stop on the tourist route for many mainlanders visiting the 'blue sea' and 'white beaches' of the 'island paradise', preserving the prefectural memory of the risky role played by the bases in the post-war era as well as of the Okinawan experience in the battle pose a challenge in nurturing a local identity in the context of the prefecture's commitment to peace (Okuda 2012, pp. 183–213). As a survey of middle school and high school students in Yaeyama revealed in June 2014, however, knowledge of the Battle of Okinawa and other aspects of the war is high, at over 90 per cent, indicating the effectiveness of peace education in passing on the memory of the war and inculcating an Okinawan identity in the younger generation (*Yaeyama Mainichi*, 22 June 2014; 25 June 2014).

Whilst much of the extant literature on contested memory explores the contestation between official (national) and grassroots (popular) memories (see below), the purpose of this article is to take up the case of Okinawa in order to shed light on the contestation between collective memories on different spatial scales, the national and subnational. More specifically, the article investigates the link between the memories of the Battle of Okinawa and US military accidents in the prefecture, on the one hand, and the appeals to reduce the US military presence, on the other, highlighting in the process the differences between the official memory at the national and prefectural levels. It focuses on how the memory of postwar US aircraft accidents in the prefecture has been linked to the memory of the Battle of Okinawa and the potential for future accidents, tying together the risk and increasing harm posed by the American military presence to the victimization of the prefecture and the everyday security of its residents.

The second section starts out by examining collective memory and the contestation of collective memory in order to set the scene for the case of Okinawa. The third section then moves on to the collective memory of the Battle of Okinawa by examining how the war has been represented in the national and local collective memories, focusing in particular on the controversy surrounding how the battle is represented in the Prefectural Peace Museum and the annual Okinawa Memorial Day. The fourth section turns to the case of the 1959 crash of an F-100 jet-fighter into the Miyamori elementary school. It illustrates how the accident remains as a powerful memory at the collective level in Okinawa. The fifth section demonstrates how the risk of harm from aircraft accidents in the post-occupation era still continues today by taking up the 2004 crash of a CH-53D transport helicopter into the grounds of Okinawa International University. Although this did not lead to any casualties among the local population, the accident yet again highlighted the ongoing risk posed to everyday security by the US military presence in the prefecture. The Conclusion summarizes the findings and reflects on the meaning of contested memory in Okinawa.

2. Collective memory and contestation

'Collective memory' is employed in this article as a heuristic device to investigate the role of the state and other agents in constructing, embedding and disseminating memory on two spatial scales, the national and the subnational, that is, the prefectural level of Okinawa. Collective memory studies normally refer to the collectivity on the national scale, with other concepts such as 'public' or 'official' memory (Olick 2003; Halbwachs 1980, 1992) and 'popular' or 'grassroots' memory (Cohen 2014) refining how memory can be conceptualized. Whilst the former takes from the concept of collective memory the role of the state in constructing, embedding and disseminating memory at the national level, and the latter the potential divergence of official memory and popular memory through grassroots contestation, conjoining them highlights how memory on these two scales of collectivity may be contested, too. Indeed, collective memory may be inherently always contested, given the different agents involved in the politically charged task of negotiating and constructing memory. Common to both scales of memory, however, is the link between the shared memory of the collectivity and collective identity (Hirst and Manier 2008). What this means is that, on both the national and subnational levels, a range of agents deploy social and political praxis to construct a plurality of memories, which are contested and negotiated in the process of their embedding and dissemination. In other words, the meaning and representation of collective memory is contested on different scales of memory construction in the process of identity formation.

In the case of Japan, this contestation has revolved around the state's attempt to embed in the national collectivity an interpretation of the empire's role in the Asia-Pacific war that downplays, obfuscates or even omits reference to the darker side of the military's war-time actions. Illustrative of this is the role of the state in approving nationalist interpretations of the war in Japanese school textbooks, as in the case of the Ministry of Education, Culture, Sports, Science and Technology's (MEXT) certification of the textbooks produced from 2001 by *Atarashii Rekishi Kyōkasho or Tsukuru Kai* (Japanese Society for History Textbook Reform) and from 2009 by textbooks produced by another nationalist group, *Kyōkasho Kaizen no Kai* (Society for Textbook Improvement) (for details, see Cave 2013). Theses state-certified school textbooks have been contested in term of their interpretation of Japan's war in China, the use of 'sex-slaves' or so-called 'comfort women' by imperial forces, the general portrayal of Japanese colonialism in Korea, and so on (Rose 1998; Soh 2008; Cave 2013).

Opposition to such nationalist endeavours to reshape the memory of the war have been contested domestically between the state and the grassroots as well as between the national and prefectural collectivities. Academics, civic groups and activists have sought to disseminate information on the war in order to erode an official narrative paying scant or no attention to Japanese crimes and atrocities. Their actions have included the recording of oral histories giving testimony to Japanese aggression, excavating government and other documents to provide evidence of how comfort women were recruited for the troops, and in general seeking to embed in the popular memory of the war the victims of Japanese aggression. Their efforts help to consolidate a popular memory that contests the official memory of the war promoted by these nationalist textbooks and nationalist politicians (Szczepanska 2014). Similar efforts have been made on the international scale, especially in China and South Korea, where protests by the state, media and the grassroots complement and supplement the efforts expended by domestic forces to provide evidence of the role of Japan as an aggressor. In this way, the negotiation and interpretation of the memory of the war between Japan and its neighbours continue to inform and constrain the official interpretation of the Asia-Pacific war. Such foreign contestation of the nationalist view of the war in Japan can be invoked on the international institutional level as well, as illustrated in June 2014 when the Chinese government submitted an application to preserve historical documents on the 'comfort women' discovered in China as part of UNESCO's Memory of the World Register (*People's Daily*, 12 June 2014).

Another issue highlighting the contestation over the memory of the war has been the role of a number of prime ministers in paying homage to the war dead at Yasukuni Shrine. The shrine hosts the Yūshūkan museum glorifying the memory of the war and, from 1978 onwards, has interred the souls of fourteen class-A war criminals convicted by the International Military Tribunal for the Far East (Breen 2008; Kingston 2010; Shimada 2014). Prime Minister Abe Shinzō's visit to Yasukuni shrine in December 2013 provoked unexpected 'disappointment' from the US as well as the expected protest from China and South Korea (*Tokyo Shimbun*, 26 December 2013). Such reactions underscore the contestation between the nationalist memory of the war promoted by the shrine and the two nationalist textbook groups mentioned above, on the one hand, and the international memory of the war, not only in East Asia, but more broadly, on the other, as elucidated in Lukner's article on contested memory related to the International Military Tribunal for the Far East in this Special Issue.

Whilst the contestation of memory across the boundaries of the state highlights how disputes over history arise between different national collectivities, and the divergence between official memory and popular memory of the war alerts us to the complex interaction between the construction of state and grassroots memories, the case of Okinawa highlights the under-explored area of political contestation on two different scales of collectivity, the national and the subnational. The point can be instanced by the controversy between the national and Okinawan collectivities in the case of the Abe government's decision to commemorate 28 April as Sovereignty Restoration Day for the first time in 2013. As far as Okinawa is concerned, commemorating the restoration of sovereignty on the date the Allied Occupation of Japan formally ended on 28 April 1952 is to commemorate a day of humiliation (*kutsujoku no hi*) as the American Occupation did not end on that day for the prefecture, but instead continued for another twenty years until Okinawa reverted to Japan in May 1972 (*Okinawa Taimuzu*, 30 April 2014). Thus, in a political snub, only the deputy-governor, not the governor, of Okinawa attended the ceremony in Tokyo and grassroots protests took place in the prefecture against the commemorative event (*Shimbun Akahata*, 29 April 2013). As this point illustrates clearly, memory is contested not only between official and popular memory, but also between the national and the prefectural, as these different scales of collectivity construct, embed and disseminate their different memories of the war and occupation.

Of course, this reference to the subnational collective memory in Okinawa does not take into account the plurality of memories in the prefecture itself, as in the different experiences and memories of the war in the main islands compared with outlying islands such as the Yaeyama island chain (Jahana 2008; Miyara 2008, pp. 163-84; *Yaeyama Mainichi*, 22 June 2014). Nor is the distinction between the national and the prefectural collectivities meant to suggest total amnesia of the war in Okinawa at the level of the national collectivity, as this is clearly not the case. For instance, an editorial in the *Tokyo Shimbun* on Okinawa Memorial Day 2014 shines a spotlight on the plight of the prefecture: 'Today is Okinawa Memorial Day. In the last great war Okinawa was sacrificed for the defence of the main islands. In the postwar era, too, it has been forced to shoulder the heavy burden of US military bases. This is the unchanging formula of making a sacrifice of the people of Okinawa' (23 June 2014). Indeed, even from before the reversion of Okinawa to Japan, writers such as Ōe Kensaburō and others have promoted greater awareness in the main islands of the impact of the war on the prefecture as have monthly journals such as *Sekai* (Ōe 1970). This means that no simple division can be drawn between the memory of the war on the national and subnational scales: interpretations and memories of the war are complex, and many on the main islands of Japan are well aware of, and indeed critical of, the activities of imperial troops in Okinawa. Nevertheless, the role of these military instruments of the imperial state in denying, eroding and compromising the security of the prefectural population, instead of providing it, remains to this day highly contested. The point can be illustrated by the 2005 court case brought against Ōe as the author of *Okinawa No-to* (1970, Okinawa note), as well as other authors and the publisher Iwanami. The plaintiffs, who launched the suit on behalf of a number of Japanese military leaders in the Battle of Okinawa, challenged the work of Ōe and the other authors showing that imperial troops 'forced' the 'group suicide' of Okinawan civilians. Following the decision of the lower courts, the Osaka High Court ruled against the plaintiffs in 2011 on the grounds that these authors had sufficient grounds to believe that the troops had indeed played such a role in the group suicides of Okinawans (see Ōe Kensaburō, Iwanami Shoten 2011). Thus, by focusing specifically on the subnational scale of collective memory we are able to shed a penetrating light on the wider contestation of memory in Japan, going beyond the division between official and grassroots memory and illuminating how a range of agents negotiate the construction, embedding and dissemination of memories at the subnational level in contrast to the national.

3. Contesting the past, linking the past to the present

One way to explore this contestation between memory on the national and the prefectural levels is to take up the case of the Battle of Okinawa. It is an ever-present memory in the prefecture, linking the past to the present, but of limited salience at the level of the national collectivity. It serves to conjoin the memory of Okinawa as a victim of the war in the past as well as a victim of the American bases in the prefecture in the present. As the only land battle fought in Japan during the Asia-Pacific war with a large civilian population, the death and destruction resulting from the battle was experienced first-hand by the locals. Although the exact number is not known, the battle is believed to have led to the death of over 100,000 Okinawan civilians, with more civilians dying than military personnel in the 'typhoon of steel and bombs' (Nakasone 1984, p. xi; Ōta 1984). The Cornerstone of Peace (*heiwa no ishiji*) is the symbol of the prefecture's annual commemoration of the battle. It was erected in the Peace Memorial Park in Mabuni, Itoman city, to commemorate the fiftieth anniversary of the end of the

Battle of Okinawa in 1995. The cornerstone 'seeks to convey Okinawa's spirit of peace ... to the people of Japan and throughout the world. The names of all those who lost their lives in the Battle of Okinawa, military and civilian alike regardless of nationality, are inscribed on the Cornerstone of Peace as a prayer for eternal peace' (Peace Memorial Park, n.d.).

Mabuni is the location where the Japanese military fought at the last stage of the battle and a large number of Okinawan civilians lost their lives. More than 241,000 names are now inscribed on the Cornerstone of Peace,[2] thousands of them civilians killed in the onslaught by American forces. What must be noted, however, is that the loss of civilian lives during the battle was due not just to the actions of enemy forces but also to those of imperial Japanese troops, who on occasion pressured the locals to commit group suicide (*shūdan jiketsu*), as evidenced in Ōe's *Okinawa No-to* and additional works. Others were killed on suspicion of spying for the Americans, for fear of them revealing the hiding places of Japanese troops, and so on (Hayashi 2009). Still other locals were put at risk by being forced out of the dugouts and caves (*gō*) used as hiding places by imperial troops (*Mainichi Shimbun*, 22 June 2014). The role of the imperial forces in targeting local civilians in this way has meant that, in the memory of the battle at the subnational level, Okinawans as victims of the Japanese as well as of the American militaries is salient. This contrasts sharply with the official memory on the national scale of collectivity, where the salience of victimhood revolves around the role of the American military, especially in dropping the atomic bombs on Hiroshima and Nagasaki.

The contestation of memory on different scales of collectivity remains at heart political. This means that, within Okinawa, supporters of the official memory promoted on the national level have played a role in challenging and seeking to erode the Okinawan collective memory. This issue has grown in salience as the generation with first-hand experience of the war has become a smaller and smaller percentage of the prefectural population as time passes. In this situation, local museums take on added significance as a means to shape the subnational memory of the Battle of Okinawa, with school children, as well as adults, being exposed to a specific interpretation of the war through the exhibitions on display. The point is illustrated by the divergent views to surface over how to represent the Battle of Okinawa in the new Prefectural Peace Memorial Museum, which was constructed during the tenure of the progressive governor of Okinawa, Ōta Masahide. The museum was being prepared for opening at the time of Ōta's electoral defeat following his unsuccessful campaign for a third term in office in December 1998. The new museum became the centre of controversy following the victory of the conservative, pro-central government challenger, Inamine Keiichi. The contestation over how to represent the battle arose due to the different views of the Inamine administration and the committee responsible for setting up the museum exhibitions. The committee sought to represent the subnational collective memory rather than the national, official memory of the battle, which diminishes, obfuscates or ignores the role of the imperial forces in causing civilian deaths. In other words, the defeat of Ōta and the election of Inamine brought to the fore how electoral victory and the change in prefectural governance from the progressives to the conservatives was of crucial importance in the politics of memory in the prefecture. Would the exhibitions in the new prefectural museum represent Okinawan or official memory?

The contestation between these two divergent memories emerged shortly after the new governor took office, when his administration disputed how the battle, the war more generally as well as the American presence in the prefecture, should be represented in the museum and instituted a number of changes in the face of the exhibition committee's strong objections. The dispute involved issues such as the inscription on the cornerstone of the names of all of those who lost their lives in the battle, whether friend or foe, combatant or non-combatant; the role of imperial soldiers in the Battle of Okinawa, including their impact on the local population; changes to how the American presence in the prefecture was represented in the post-war era, taking up the consequences of the bases for Okinawans, and so on (Yonetani 2000, 2001). One of the most highly charged parts of the exhibition was a diorama related to the Battle of Okinawa. Originally, the diorama was set up in such a way as to show a Japanese soldier with his rifle pointing at a local mother with babe in arms, alluding to how the soldier might take action against them, fearing the noise of the infant crying could alert the enemy to their whereabouts. In an oral history project later launched by the *Ryūkyū Shimpō*, a child at the time of the battle relates a similar incident when hiding with her mother in a cave. The mother was holding her younger sibling, which started to cry. The Japanese soldier reacted by threatening: 'if you don't get out of here I'll use my weapon' (*teppo de yaru yo*) (*Ryūkyū Shimpō Recording*, 10 September 2011). After the election of the new governor, the diorama was changed radically so that in the version put on display the soldier's rifle is held in such a way as to represent him protecting instead of threatening the mother. Clearly, the politics of memory is fought out within Okinawa as well as between the national and subnational collectivities, with the Inamine administration aligned more with the official, national representation of the war than the Ōta administration, which placed emphasis on representing the memory of Okinawans. In this way, the election of the new conservative governor in place of Ōta transformed the way the prefectural museum displayed the role of imperial soldiers in the battle, demonstrating the importance of exploring how memory is contested at the national-subnational as well as official-grassroots levels.

In addition to the role of the Prefectural Peace Museum in memory politics, the Battle of Okinawa has become part of the prefectural collective memory as a result of an annual memorial service commemorating the ending of the battle on 23 June 1945. It was first held during the American occupation, in 1952. Known as the Okinawan Memorial Service for all of the war dead (*Okinawa zen senbotsu sha tsuitō shikiten*), it is recognized as a national holiday in the prefecture, the *irei no hi* (Okinawa Memorial Day, literally, the day to console the spirits). A one-minute silence is held at noon. With the reversion of Okinawa to Japan in 1972, the Memorial Day was no longer officially recognized as a holiday under Japanese law, although 23 June continued to be honoured as such at the local level. With the 1991 revision of the local autonomy law (*chihōjichihō*), moreover, a prefectural ordinance was passed to make 23 June an official holiday again. The prefecture and other public facilities such as schools close for the day. Whilst the memorial's ostensible purpose is to remember the war and to call for everlasting peace, it at the same time plays a crucial role in the politics of memory in the prefecture. The point is illustrated by the way local policy-makers and other subnational actors construct a link between the memory of the war and the existence and operation of US bases in the prefecture and the risk these outposts of American power pose to the everyday security of the local population.

At the commemoration in 2013, for instance, governor Nakaima Hirokazu made the annual 'peace declaration' (*heiwa sengen*) in which he called on the Abe administration to 'move the Futenma base outside of the prefecture as quickly as possible,' as he had done in the previous two years following his election in November 2010 (*Tokyo Shimbun*, 19 June 2013). In the following year, on Okinawa Memorial Day in June 2014, the governor included this request in the declaration once again, and added that he is 'calling for the halt to the operation of Marine Corps Air Station Futenma within five years' (*Mainichi Shimbun*, 23 June 2014). Rumours had circulated earlier in the month that the governor would not follow his previous three declarations in calling for the Futenma base to be relocated outside of the prefecture. The inclusion of his appeal to halt the base's operations within five years followed the governor's decision at the end of 2013 to approve the land-fill off the costal part of Henoko in preparation for the transfer of the Futenma base to the proposed new site (*Okinawa Taimuzu*, 28 December 2012). At the time, the governor declared that, even though he had approved the land-fill, he still favoured the relocation of the Futenma base outside of the prefecture – 'a logic without logic,' as dubbed in an editorial by the *Okinawa Taimuzu* (11 June 2014). In any event, by repeating his earlier appeal to move the base out of the prefecture he faced less risk of alienating the voters in the November 2014 election for governor, although in the end his re-election bid failed.

Similarly, other speakers have used the occasion of the Okinawa Memorial Day to promote a political agenda seeking to change the status quo of the US bases in the prefecture. At the 2013 event, for instance, Kina Masaharu, president of the prefectural assembly (*kengikaigichō*), linked the memory of the Battle of Okinawa with the bases and called for the relocation of Futenma outside of the prefecture as Okinawans were at 'the limits of their endurance' (*Ryūkyū Shimpō*, 24 June 2013). At the memorial service in June 2014, moreover, Kina again brought up the issue of the bases, this time highlighting how the US military's 'forced' deployment of the MV-22 Osprey tilt-rotor aircraft and other actions represented the 'countless times the democratic will of the people of Okinawa has been crushed. The distrust of and anger against the national government has reached its limit' (*Ryūkyū Shimpō*, 23 June 2014).³ Further, the chair of the War-Bereaved Families Association, Okinawa Branch (*izoku rengōkai*), Teruya Naeko, attended the memorial service in 2013 and spoke in opposition to the deployment of the Osprey in her role as a bearer of the memory of the bereaved families, saying 'as bereaved families we can never accept' them (*Ryūkyū Shimpō*, 24 June 2013). In 2014, she called for the relocation of the Futenma base outside of the prefecture (*Ryūkyū Shimpō*, 24 June 2014).

As in the case of the 2013 and 2014 memorial services, these declarations and speeches are frequently made in front of the serving prime minister, underscoring their role as part of the politics of memory in Okinawa. The first prime minister to attend the memorial service was Prime Minister Kaifu Toshiki in 1990.⁴ Ten different prime ministers have attended the service between 1990 and 2014.⁵ The current prime minister, Abe Shinzō, was in attendance during his inaugural administration in 2007 as well as in both 2013 and 2014. In 2013 he was joined for the first time by the foreign minister and the minister of defence. The two were by his side again in 2014. What this means is that, in speeches made on the day, local officials and others can deploy the local memory of the war as a political resource to highlight current Okinawan problems and the local political agenda in front of the prime minister and other national officials. In other words, by linking together the Battle of Okinawa and the continuing suffering of the people as a result of the concentration of US military installations in the prefecture, their speeches help to embed and disseminate the memory of the war, thereby linking together the past and the present victimization of the prefecture.

In 2013, Prime Minister Abe did not bring up US bases in his own speech, but in media interviews afterwards he highlighted how 'the concentration of US bases is a major burden on prefectural residents. I will do my best to lessen this even a little' (*Ryūkyū Shimpō*, 24 June 2013). His greetings in 2014 included a similar sentiment to do his best to reduce the burden of the bases in Okinawa (*Mainichi Shimbun*, 23 June 2014). From the local perspective, however, many saw the prime minister's motivation in making these statements as nothing more than an attempt to gain popular acquiescence in the relocation of the Futenma base to Henoko. As one Okinawan who had lost her parents in the war put it to the *Okinawa Taimuzu* in 2013: 'It is unnatural for so many [ministers] to abruptly turn up. It's no doubt because of Futenma and [the deployment of] the Ospreys' (24 June 2013). Another said national leaders come along and 'superficially express a sympathetic attitude and try to get on well with us, but the continuing heavy burden of the bases throughout the post-war period is the same as discrimination against Okinawa' (*Okinawa Taimuzu*, 24 June 2013). This promise to reduce the burden on Okinawa is nothing new for the prime ministers of Japan, irrespective of political party, as evidenced in the greetings made by the Democratic Party of Japan Prime Minister, Noda Yoshihiko, in 2012: 'I am overwhelmed with shame from the reality of the concentration of US bases in Okinawa even now and the great burden these have placed for many years on the people of the prefecture. I will do my best to reduce the burden of the bases at an early stage and I once again vow to push forward with this in concrete ways visible to all' (Prime Minister's Office 2012). Despite these commitments, however, the burden of the existence and operation of US bases in Okinawa continues as before, suggesting how the memory of the war still has a role to play in the politics of memory, with prefectural officials and others seeking to improve the local situation by highlighting the link between the Battle of Okinawa and the ongoing US presence in the prefecture.

4. Crash at Miyamori elementary school

Another way the past is linked to the risk posed to the everyday security of the citizens by the current presence of US facilities in the prefecture is by constructing, embedding and disseminating the memory of military accidents caused by the operation of the bases at the subnational level as well as more widely. For the local population, US installations are not simply a matter of the location of foreign military outposts in Okinawa in order to shore up the abstract notion of deterrence. Their existence and operation are rather a risk to the everyday security of the inhabitants, as evidenced by the crash of a US fighter-jet into the Miyamori elementary school in 1959. The case illustrates how the continued suffering of Okinawans is linked to the deployment of the US military as well as to the call for the reduction or elimination of the US presence in the prefecture. The point was made clearly by the head teacher of the school when he gave his condolences at a ceremony two days after the crash: 'Is this acceptable? Despite the war having already ended fifteen years ago, I think this is a major tragedy for the people (*minzoku*) who live on an island of bases' (*Ryūkyū Shimpō*, 2 July 1959). Although the accident occurred during the American occupation, the Okinawan collective memory of the event remains strong in the post-occupation era, too, as the results of a 2007 prefectural survey affirm: the accident was listed as the seventh most important event in the history of Okinawa (pollees chose three events) (*Ryūkyū Shimpō* 2007, p. 36).

The crash occurred on 30 June 1959 when an F-100 fighter from the US's Kadena Air Base crashed into the sixth-district of Ichikawa (now Urama) city and then continued to travel across the ground and engulf the Miyamori (now Urama) elementary school. The pilot ejected from the plane following the explosion of the engine. It was first reported that he had dumped his payload over the sea, but later reports based on American sources state four bombs were still aboard the fighter when it crashed (*Ryūkyū Shimpō*, 30 June 1999). The accident led to the death of seventeen, eleven school children and six residents, as well as the injury of 210, over 150 children and more than 50 residents. Five of those who were killed had lived through the Battle of Okinawa, with the remainder born after the war. Twenty-seven homes, one community centre and three classrooms were burned to the ground. Eight homes and two classrooms were partially destroyed and a kindergarten could no longer be used due to the damage suffered. The source of the crash was later revealed to be human error in maintaining the plane. On hearing this, a bereaved mother who had lost her eldest daughter as a result of the accident, stated: 'flying a jet without carrying out proper maintenance is outrageous. It seems [the US military] does not regard Okinawans as people' (*Ryūkyū Shimpō*, 30 June 1999).

The memory of the event has been constructed, embedded and disseminated by the actions of the school, the bereaved families, classmates from the time, graduates of the school and others. To start with, the accident is commemorated in the grounds of the school by a copper plaque of the garden deity for the protection of children, *nakayoshi jizō*, which was erected on the anniversary of the accident in June 1965 (for an image, see Inochi to Heiwa no Kataribe, 2011, p. 5). It is based on a drawing by the novelist and artist, Mushanokoji Saneatsu, who sent his contribution following the request of a priest in Tokyo. The memory of the crash is embedded among the pupils at the school through the plaque as well as a memorial service held annually at the school on 30 June. Local political leaders join the school children, teachers and others at this event. In 2012, for instance, the mayor of Uruma city made a speech linking the memory of the accident to the present-day concern about US forces in Okinawa, raising his voice in opposition to the deployment of the Osprey in the prefecture (*Ryūkyū Shimpō*, 1 July 2012).

At the same time, local leaders, former pupils and others have sought to disseminate the memory of the accident in other parts of Japan as well as in the prefecture. This can be seen, for instance, in the case of the mayor of Ginowan, who gave a talk about the tragedy on the fifty-first anniversary of the crash in August 2010 at the civic centre in Bunkyō ward, Tokyo. Pupils, former pupils and young people from the surrounding area put on a play of the event on the fiftieth anniversary of the accident, *Fukugi no Shizuku* (*dew of the common garcinia*).[6] It was staged locally and later in Tokyo. Others have spread the memory of the accident more widely. For instance, on the fortieth anniversary of Okinawa's reversion to Japan in 2012, the crash provided the material for a movie, *Himawari – Okinawa wa wasurenai ano hi no sora o* (*Sunflower: the sky on the day Okinawa does not forget*), released in 2013. Although the film is a fictional human drama, not a documentary, the story highlights the ongoing risk posed by the operation of the bases by conjoining the memory of the 1959 crash at Miyamori school and the 2004 crash of the Marine Corps Air Station Futenma's CH-53D Sea Stallion into Okinawa International University (discussed below). In this way, the film relates Okinawa's continuing suffering as a result of the bases by linking US military accidents from both the occupation and post-occupation eras to the risk posed to everyday security by the concentration of US military installations in the prefecture to this day.

With the appointment of a head teacher who was a pupil at the school at the time of the crash, the fiftieth anniversary of the accident in 2009 provided an opportunity for those involved in embedding and disseminating the memory of the accident to expand their role. This is illustrated by the ongoing efforts being made to collect memorabilia from the bereaved families, such as the victims' school work and playthings as well as portraits of the deceased and other images related to the crash. The aim is to display them in a permanent exhibition or museum of the tragedy (*Ryūkyū Shimpō*, 30 June 2009). Such local efforts to deploy artefacts as a means to preserve the memory of the Miyamori crash were given concrete form that year by the creation of a non-profit organization (NPO), the Ishikawa Miyamori 630 (Inochi to Heiwa no Kataribe 2009). The head teacher was joined by other survivors amongst the pupils and teachers as well as the bereaved families and others interested in raising funds and carrying out activities in order to embed the memory of the crash by constructing the Ishikawa Miyamori 630 Hall (*kan*) as a site for permanent commemoration.

The group's dissemination activities have included the creation in 2009 of a travelling exhibition of photographs of the accident. At the display in the Ginowan city office the then mayor, Iha Yōhei, linked the memory of the Miyamori crash to the ongoing risk of another military accident taking place in the prefecture: 'Even today, fifty years later, a US military accident can occur anywhere. The travelling exhibition of the 630 group offers us a great opportunity to take another hard look at the present situation of Okinawa' (*Ginowan Shihō* 2009, p. 9). In a later exhibition in 2012, the deputy mayor of Ginowan, Matsukawa Masanori, linked the exhibition of the accident with the crash at Okinawa International University, the recent deployment of the Osprey in the prefecture and the ongoing struggle against the US military bases: 'The city has taken on board the latest warning of the crash of the US helicopter at Okinawa International University, and we are tackling the early closure and return of the Futenma air station as well as the reversal of the deployment of the Ospreys. I am grateful for the creation of a place where we can disseminate a message opposed to these deployments' (*Ginowan Shihō* 2012, p. 9).

At the same time as gathering objects and images related to the crash and holding photo exhibitions of the tragedy, the 630 group launched an oral history project to collect and disseminate the memories of those at the school at the time. The victims' families, teachers and classmates have started to speak out, offering first-hand testimony of the accident published in three volumes (Inochi to Heiwa no Kataribe 2010, 2011, 2011a). The memories demonstrate the way the response to the crash was a joint effort involving the local residents, especially the parents of the pupils at the school, as well as the American military. As one of the teachers states as she remembers the day: 'I checked what had happened to the children in my class one at a time. Had they been evacuated? Who had been taken to hospital? After a while I could no longer lift my arm. It seems the window frame had flown through the air and hit my left shoulder. An American

(*America san*) spotted my injury and took me by ambulance to the military hospital' (Higa n.d. Also see Inochi to Heiwa no Kataribe 2010, pp. 16–17). Another of the surviving teachers linked the memory of the crash to the present situation in Okinawa: 'Whatever amount of compensation is received, however often apologies are given, the feelings of the bereaved families do not change. As long as US military bases remain in Okinawa, there will never be absolute security. In order for us not to experience such grief again, I think we should make Okinawa an island of peace' (Shinzatō 1997. Also see Inochi to Heiwa no Kataribe 2010, pp. 20–21).

5. Crash at Okinawa International University

Another way the past has been linked to the US military presence in Okinawa has been to preserve the memory of other serious accidents to occur in the post-Occupation period alongside that of Miyamori. Whilst the crash of the US fighter into the elementary school was the most serious accident to occur during the American Occupation of Okinawa and indeed in the post-war period as a whole, other military accidents have taken place during the years following the prefecture's reversion to Japan in 1972. The memories of other serious accidents have been constructed, embedded and disseminated at the subnational level, as illustrated by the case of the August 2004 crash of a helicopter from the Futenma Marine Corps Air Station, the CH-53D Sea Stallion, into the main building (*honkan*) of Okinawa International University in Ginowan city. The accident occurred a few hundred metres from the fence dividing the university and the Futenma air station when the pilot lost control of the Sea Stallion during a military exercise. One of the helicopter's six blades snapped off the rotor and flew several hundred metres into the street outside of the campus after striking the main building of the university. The other blades then struck the ground and building and the CH-53D burst into flames, causing thick black smoke to rise up to ten metres into the sky. Debris such as concrete from the building and bits from the helicopter were strewn far beyond the university's environs. Although the crash happened during the summer recess, over seven hundred students and members of the administrative and academic staff were on campus at the time, some escaping harm as a result of being behind the pillars of the main building at the time of the impact. Housing is located close by and pedestrians and vehicles were on the streets next to the campus. The university president contextualized the meaning of the crash to the university and local community in a presentation shortly after the accident at the Commission on the Review of Overseas Military Facility Structure of the United States: 'When the helicopter collided with the building, the main rotor hit the wall and shot numerous chunks of concrete in many directions beyond the campus, as far as a quarter of a mile away. It is a true miracle that they killed nobody' (Okinawa International University, n.d.).

One of the key points of difference between the crash at the Miyamori elementary school during the occupation and the crash into Okinawa International University in the post-occupation years is how the Status of Force Agreement between the US and Japan works in practice (the agreement was applied to Okinawa after reversion), particularly in constraining the role of local officials in responding to the risk posed by US aircraft when manifest as harm (Hook *et al.* 2015; Honma *et al.* 2001; Honma 1996). Of course, as we saw in the case of the crash at Miyamori, where one of the victims recalled the role of 'America san' in taking her to the military hospital, the Americans are represented in the memory of the earlier event. But what is critical about how the memory of the crash at the university has been constructed, embedded and disseminated at the subnational level is the salience of the role of the US military in its aftermath. The marines imposed a cordon on the university for four days, so not only the staff, students and the curious but also the police and other local officials were barred from entering the campus, preventing them from investigating the accident. The US forces then took the step to re-start flights by the Sea Stallion, even though the cause of the accident had not been disclosed to the Japanese side. The way the US acted at the time has been constructed, embedded and disseminated in local memory as a representation of how Okinawa continues to suffer as a victim of the US military (Kurosawa 2005). In essence, the prefecture is represented as still being under American occupation in the memory of the crash.

The fifth anniversary of the accident in 2009 coincided with the fiftieth anniversary of the crash at Miyamori. Thus, 2009 offered a narrative device to link the memory of the two crashes together in opposition to the continuing US military presence in Okinawa. The twin anniversaries served to bolster the efforts made by members of the faculty and students to preserve the memory of the crash at the university (Ishikawa 2010; Kurosawa 2005, pp. 164–267). For the prefecture as a whole, the accident confirmed the inherent risk of a base located in the midst of a city. It reinforced the reason for wanting to move the Futenma base out of a crowded city and affirmed the description of Futenma given by the then US Secretary of Defense, Donald Rumsfeld, on a visit to Okinawa the year before the helicopter came down: 'the world's most dangerous base' (*Ryūkyū Shimpō*, 13 August 2013).

Meanwhile, local political leaders have expressed concern about the lack of progress on the implementation of the SACO agreement and the relocation of 'the world's most dangerous base' from Ginowan. For instance, the Ginowan city mayor, Sakima Atsushi, linked the memory of the crash at the university to the ongoing issue of the failure to implement the agreement to close down Futenma (Ginowan city 2013). In this way, the memory of military accidents can be used by local leaders as well as activists as a political resource to mount resistance to US bases in the prefecture. Still, this resistance, built up over many years (Tanji 2006; McCormack and Oka Norimatsu 2012), is not simply a reaction to contemporaneous military base issues. Rather, resistance is nurtured by the memory of what has occurred in the past, as in the case of the crashes at Miyamori elementary school and Okinawa International University as well as heinous crimes committed by US military personnel, as in the case of the 1995 rape of a twelve-year old school girl by three American soldiers (Angst 2003; Okuda 2012, pp. 241–274).

To this end, both staff and students have sought to preserve the evidence of the crash as a site for commemoration as well as carrying out activities to embed and disseminate the memory of the event. As an example, students, faculty and others launched a range of activities to preserve the external 'black wall' (*kuroi kabe*) of the main building, which had been blackened by the smoke of the flames rising from the helicopter. The students carried out a signature campaign, collecting over 5000 signatures from both inside and outside of the university to put pressure on the university administration to preserve the wall. These were presented to the president with an appeal to leave the wall in its present condition so that the memory of the accident would 'not be allowed to disappear' (*fūka sasenai*) (*Shimbun Akahata*, 8 October 2004). The wall is viewed as a concrete manifestation of the crash and as a symbol of the risk posed to everyday security by the planes and helicopters flying over Ginowan. These sentiments became part of the memory of the crash for a neighbour overlooking the site, who kept her curtains closed for nearly ten months afterwards (*Ryūkyū Shimpō*, 11 August 2005). In the end, however, the cost of repairing and maintaining the site as well as the lack of space on campus meant the university administration decided to demolish the building and construct a replacement. Instead of the preservation of the 'black wall' as a way to commemorate the crash, the university decided to establish a commemorative monument.

At the same time, the staff and students have been working to construct, embed and disseminate the memory of the crash by holding exhibitions, symposia, commemorative events, and so on. In 2007, for instance, a photographic exhibition was held as part of the 'no fly zone concert' put on by the students (*Ryūkyū Shimpō*, 8 August 2007). In order to pass on the memory to the next generation, school children were brought to see the exhibition. In 2014, on the tenth anniversary of the crash, the faculty in the Okinawa Law and Politics Research Centre (Okinawa Hōsei Kenkyūjo) hosted lectures and a symposium in commemoration on the theme of Okinawan identity (Okinawa Hōsei Kenkyūjo 2014). On the commemorative day in August to celebrate the tenth anniversary, moreover, the university organized a 'meeting to think about Okinawa from the perspective of Futenma,' at which the president demanded the immediate closure of the base (*Nihon Keizai Shimbun*, 14 August, 2014). A mother, who had been a student at the time of the crash, participated with her son and 'renewed her idea of wanting to pass on the reality of the accident to future generations' (*Nihon Keizai Shimbun*, 14 August, 2014). Finally, recognizing the role of art in embedding and disseminating the memory of the crash, a local artist produced a work using the crash at Okinawa International University as his inspiration, as he 'did not want the memory of the accident to disappear' and 'does not want US bases in Okinawa' (*Okinawa Taimuzu*, 13 August 2014).

6. Conclusion

In this way, excavating the power of memory by exploring the study of the politics of contested memory in Okinawa adds value to the extant literature by elucidating how memory diverges at the level of the national and subnational collectivities, whilst at the same time underscoring how 'official' memory in Okinawa aligns overwhelmingly with popular memory. Of course, memory is still contested between the progressive and conservative forces in Okinawa, as seen in the case of the Inamine administration's intervention to promote the national official memory in the exhibition on the Battle of Okinawa at the Prefectural Peace Memorial Museum. But both progressive and conservative forces share a common goal of reducing, if not eliminating, US bases in Okinawa. The experience of the Battle of Okinawa and the risk to everyday security posed by the US presence has led a range of actors to carry out activities in order to construct, embed and disseminate the memories of the battle as well as the military accidents at Miyamori elementary school and Okinawa International University. Still, these collective memories on the national and prefectural scales do not simply represent the construction, embedding and dissemination of two different memories, but an interaction between the two, played out through negotiation and contestation. This process leads to a changing field of memory, as illustrated by the exhibition at the prefectural peace museum and the representation of the Japanese soldier and his weapon.

The Okinawa Memorial Day provides the opportunity for Okinawans to remember those who lost their lives in the war. This function of commemoration is supplemented and complemented by the ongoing concern with the risks posed to everyday security by US bases in the prefecture. The point is illustrated by the way local political leaders and others linked their speeches at the memorial service to remember the Battle of Okinawa to the continuing role of the American eagle in the prefecture. The memory of the war provides local leaders with a political resource to link the battle to the bases in front of national leaders, including the prime minister. However, connecting the memory of the past to the ongoing presence of US bases has not led to the closure or relocation of US bases outside of the prefecture, the goal of a majority of local political leaders as well as activists. What these commemorative activities provide, though, is sustenance of a separate Okinawan identity, built on the sense of being a victim of both Japan and the United States.

This identity of Okinawa as victim is reinforced by the incidents and accidents associated with the operation of US bases in the prefecture. The commemorative activities at the Miyamori elementary school have highlighted the tragic consequences of a military accident involving the loss of lives. Through their ongoing efforts the bereaved families, surviving classmates and others have constructed, embedded and disseminated the memory of the crash and now aim to institutionalize it by constructing a museum. Whether this goal is achieved or not should not divert us from the point that, by their actions to preserve the memory of the military accident at Miyamori, they have contributed to the nurturing of a different memory and identity in Okinawa to that of the national collectivity.

Meanwhile, in the case of the Sea Stallion accident at Okinawa International University, the students and staff were at the centre of an attempt to commemorate what happened by the preservation of a symbol of the crash, the 'black wall'. Clearly, the central administration differed over how to preserve the memory of the crash and in the end opted to demolish the wall. However, the negotiated compromise of a commemorative monument was not so much due to the contestation of the memory of the accident per se so much as the limited space on campus and the cost of preserving the wall. Indeed, the university community in general recognized the importance of embedding and disseminating the memory of the accident, as part of the memory of the university and of Okinawa. The difference between the two sides seems to have been more over means than ends.

Overall, what the above discussion suggests is how the memories of the Battle of Okinawa and of the two military accidents have served as one of the ingredients for nurturing an Okinawan identity based on being a victim of both Japan and of the US. The efforts made to construct, embed and disseminate the memory of what makes Okinawa different from the main islands, whether in terms of the land battle fought in Okinawa or the concentration of US military bases leading to the two crashes and the risk of future accidents, have helped to nurture this identity. Whilst the socio-political context has changed over time, the continued deployment of US forces remains as a constant reminder of the risk to everyday security posed by potential future accidents. Thus, the prefecture's struggle to move the bases outside of Okinawa is not simply a means to redress the unequal distribution of US military installations throughout Japan, but also a way to challenge the unequal treatment of the prefecture by both the national and American governments. In other words, the anti-base struggle is at heart a struggle about bringing the unfinished war to a conclusion.

Disclosure statement

No potential conflict of interest was reported by the authors.

Funding

The author is grateful to the AHRC (grant number AH/L006758/1) for funding to make this article available through open access.

Notes

1. The expression the 'unfinished war' is from an interview with one of the Antiwar Landlords, Teruya Shuden in 2007. The US bases occupying their land are a symbol of the unfinished war (see Hook 2010).
2. Names are still being added to the Cornerstone of Peace. An additional 54 names were added in 2014 making the total 241,281. (*Ryūkyū Shimpō*, 24 June 2014).
3. Twelve MV-22 Osprey tiltrotor aircraft were deployed to Marine Corp Air Station Futenma during October 2012 and eleven in 2013. The deployment led to protests in Okinawa, especially as the Osprey has a poor safety record.
4. For the speeches made by prime ministers between 1990 and 2010, see Okinawa Taimuzu (2012).
5. The prime ministers are as follows: Kaifu Toshiki (1990); Murayama Tomi'ichi (1995); Mori Toshirō (2000); Koizumi Junichirō (2001); Abe Shinzō (2007); Fukuda Yasuo (2008); Aso Tarō (2009); Kan Naoto (2010); Kan Naoto (2011); Noda Yoshihiko (2012); Abe Shinzō (2013); Abe Shinzō (2014).
6. The *Asahi Shimbun* (2 December 2011, English edition) reported that the title was selected 'because trees of the common garcinia at Miyamori Elementary School were damaged in the accident, and sap that looked like milk spilled from their trunks and branches. The sap was taken to represent the tears of the bereaved families. When the crash occurred, it was time for 'milk lunch' at the school, which provided only milk to the students who brought 'bento' lunch boxes from home.'

References

Angst, L. I., 2003. The rape of a schoolgirl: discourses of power and women's lives in Okinawa. *In*: L. Hein and M. Selden, eds. *Islands of discontent: Okinawan responses to Japanese and American power*. Lanham: Rowman and Littlefield, 135–156.

Breen, J., ed., 2008. *Yasukuni, the war dead, and the struggle for Japan's past*. New York: Columbia University Press.

Cave, P., 2013. Japanese colonialism and the Asia Pacific war in Japan's history textbooks: changing representations and their causes. *Modern Asian Studies*, 47 (2), 542–580.

Cohen, P. A., 2014. *History and popular memory. The power of story in moments of crisis*. New York: Columbia University Press

Ginowan city, 2013. Okinawa Kokusai Daigaku e no beigun CH-53D gata heri tsuiraku jiko kara 9 nen, shichō komento (The mayor's comment nine years after the crash of the United States CH-53D helicopter into Okinawa International University. Available from: http://www.city.ginowan.okinawa.jp/organization/kichisyougaika/sisei/base/05/okiuheli9nen.html [Accessed 3 June 2014].

Ginowan Shihō., 2009. November. No. 572. Available from: http://www.city.ginowan.okinawa.jp/DAT/LIB/WEB/1/121122.pdf [Accessed 9 June 2014].

Ginowan Shihō., 2012. November. No. 608. Available from: http://www.city.ginowan.okinawa.jp/DAT/LIB/WEB/1/121122.pdf [Accessed 9 June 2014].

Halbwachs, M., 1980. *The collective memory*. New York: Harper and Row Colophon Books.

Halbwachs, M., 1992. *On collective memory*. Chicago: University of Chicago Press.

Hayashi, H., 2009. *Okinawasen kyōsei sareta 'shūdan jiketsu'* (Forced 'mass suicide' in the battle of Okinawa). Tokyo: Yoshikawa kōbunkan.

Higa, S., n.d. Taikensha no shōgen (Testimony of those who experienced the crash at Miyamori). *Inochi to Heiwa no Kataribe. Ishikawa Miyamori 630 kai*. Available from: http://ishikawamiyamori630kai.cloud-line.com/syougen/higa/ [Accessed 9 June 2014].

Himeyuri Peace Museum., n.d. Available from: http://www.himeyuri.or.jp/ [Accessed 9 September 2014].

Hirst, W. and Manier, D., 2008. Towards a psychology of collective memory. *Memory*, 17, 183–200.

Honma, H., 1996. Zainichi beigun chiikyōtei (The status of forces agreement of United States forces in Japan). Tokyo: Nihon Hyōronsha.

Honma, H., Sonnenberg, D. and Timm, T. A., 2001. United States forces in Japan: a bilateral experience. *In*: D. Fleck, ed. *The handbook of the law of visiting forces*. Oxford: Oxford University Press, 365–416.

Hook, G. D., 2010. Intersecting risks and governing Okinawa: American bases and the unfinished war. *Japan Forum*, 22 (1–2), 195–217.

Hook, G. D., Mason, R. and O'Shea, P., 2015. *Regional risk and security in Japan: whither the everyday*. Abingdon: Routledge.

Inochi to Heiwa no Kataribe. Ishikawa Miyamori 630 kai, 2009. Available from: http://ishikawamiyamori630kai.cloud-line.com/ [Accessed 9 June 2014].

Inochi to Heiwa no Kataribe. Ishikawa Miyamori 630 kaihen, 2010. *Okinawa no sora no shita de. Shōgen aa kono hisan. Ishikawa Miyamori jettoki suiryaku Jiko* (Beneath the sky of Okinawa. Testimony to the tragic disaster. The crash of a jetfighter at Miyamori, Ishikawa). Vol. 1. Urama: Ishikawa Miyamori 630 kai.

Inochi to Heiwa no Kataribe. Ishikawa Miyamori 630 kaihen, 2011. *Okinawa no sora no shita de. Shōgen aa kono hisan. Ishikawa Miyamori jettoki suiryaku Jiko* (Beneath the sky of Okinawa. Testimony to the tragic disaster. The crash of a jetfighter at Miyamori, Ishikawa). Vol 2. Urama: Ishikawa Miyamori 630 kai.

Inochi to Heiwa no Kataribe. Ishikawa Miyamori 630 kaihen, 2011a. *Okinawa no sora no shita de. Shōgen aa kono hisan. Ishikawa Miyamori jettoki suiryaku Jiko* (Beneath the sky of Okinawa. Testimony to the tragic disaster. The crash of a jetfighter at Miyamori, Ishikawa). Vol 3. Urama: Ishikawa Miyamori 630 kai.

Ishikawa Zemina-ru., 2010. Ginowan, Okinawa Kokusai Daigaku beigun herikoputa- tsuiraku jiken 5 nen. Ishikawa, Miyamori shōgakko beigun jettoki tsuiraku jiken 50 nen (Ginowan, Five years after the crash at Okinawa International University. Fifty years after a United States' jet fighter crashed into Miyamori elementary school). Naha: Okinawa Kokusai Daigaku Sōgō Bunka Gakubu Shakai Bunka Gakka Ishikawa Zemina-ru.

Jahana, N., 2008. *Shōgen. Okinawa 'shūdan jiketsu'. Kerima shotō de nani ga okita ka* (Testimony. Okinawa's 'mass suicide.' What happened on the Kerima islands). Tokyo: Iwanani.

Kingston, J., 2010. Record in pictures of Yasukuni Jinja: Yushukan. *Critical Asian Studies*, 42 (3), 497–499.

Kurosawa, A., ed., 2005. *Okikokudai ga Amerika ni senryō sareta hi* (The day Okinawa International University was occupied by the United States). Tokyo: Seidosha.

McCormack, G. and Oka Norimatsu, S., 2012. *Resistant islands: Okinawa confronts Japan and the United States*. Lanham: Rowman and Littlefield.

Ministry of Foreign Affairs., 1996. Available from: http://www.mofa.go.jp/region/n-america/us/security/96saco2.html [Accessed 9 June 2014].

Miyagi, K., 1995. *Himeyuri no shōjo. 16 sai no senjō*; (A girl of the himeyuri nursing corps. The battlefield at sixteen). Tokyo: Kōbunken.

Miyara, S., 2008. *Kokkyō no shima. Yonagunitōshi: sono kindai o saguru* (Island on the border. The Yonaguni island magazine: exploring the modern era). Naha: Akebo no Shuppan.

Nakasone, S., 1984. Preface. *In*: M. Ōta, ed. *The battle of Okinawa. The typhoon of steel and bombs*. Tokyo: Kume Publishing, x–xi.

Ōe, 1970 Ōe, K., 1970. *Okinawa no-to* (Okinawa note). Tokyo: Iwanami Shoten.

Ōe Kensaburō, Iwanami Shoten [Ōe Kensaburō, Iwanami Shoten Okinawasen Saiban Shien Renryakukai. Available from: http://osaka-rekkyo.main.jp/okinawasen/ [Accessed 12 August 2014].

Okinawa Hōsei Kenkyūjo (Okinawa International University), 2014. Available from: http://oilp.okiu.ac.jp/detail.jsp?id=60138&type=TopicsTopPage&funcid=2 [Accessed 19 June 2014].

Okinawa International University, n.d. Statement by the Present of Okinawa University regarding the USMC helicopter crash and request for the closure of USMC Futenma Air Station (2004). Available from: http://oilp.okiu.ac.jp/detail.jsp?id=60138&type=TopicsTopPage&funcid=2 [Accessed 2 June 2014].

Okinawa Prefectural Government., 2013. *Okinawa no beigun kichi* (United States bases in Okinawa). Naha: Okinawa Ken Chiji Kōshitsu, Kichi Taisakuka.

Okinawa Prefectural Government, 2013a. Futenma hikōjo no kikensei (The danger of the Futenma air station). Available from: http://www.pref.okinawa.lg.jp/site/chijiko/chian/futenma/risk.html [Accessed 2 August 2014].

Okinawa Taimuzu, 2012. *Okinawa zensen botsusha tsuitō shiki. Rekidai shushō*; (The Okinawan memorial service for all of the war dead. Prime ministers' speeches). Naha: Okinawa Taimuzu.

Okuda, H., 2012. *Okinawa no kioku: 'shihai' to 'teikō' no rekishi* (Memory in Okinawa: a history of 'control' and 'resistance'). Tokyo: Keiōjigiku daigaku shuppankai.

Olick, J. K., 2003. What does it mean to normalize the past? Official memory in German politics since 1989. In: J. Olick, ed. *States of memory: continuities, conflicts and transformations in national retrospection*. Durham, NC: Duke University Press, 259–288.

Ōta, M., 1984. *The battle of Okinawa. The typhoon of steel and bombs*. Tokyo: Kume Publishing.

Peace Memorial Park., n.d. Available from: http://sp.heiwa-irei-okinawa.jp/stone/stone01.html [Accessed 19 June 2014].

Prime Minister's Office, 2012. Okinawa Zensen Botsusha Tsuitōshiki. Sōri aisatsu (The Prime Minister's greeting at the Okinawan memorial service for all of the war dead), 23 June. Available from: http://www.kantei.go.jp/jp/noda/statement/2012/okinawa_tuitousiki.html [Accessed 19 June 2014].

Rose, C., 1998. *Interpreting history in Sino-Japanese relations: a case study in political decision making*. London: Routledge.

Rothschild, E., 1995. What is security? *Daedalus*, 124 (3), 53–98.

Ryūkyū Shimpō., 2007. *Okinawa kenmin ishiki chōsa hōkokusho* (Survey report on the attitudes of the prefectural residents of Okinawa). Naha: Ryūkyū Shimpō.

Ryūkyū Shimpō Recording, 10 September 2011. Available from: http://ryukyushimpo.jp/photo/storyid-181495.html [Accessed 20 June 2014].

Shimada, H., 2014. *Yasukuni jinja* (Yasukuni shrine). Tokyo: Gentosha.

Shinzatō, R., 1997. *Taikensha no shōgen* (Testimony of those who experienced the crash at Miyamori). Available from: http://cloud-line.com/ishikawamiyamori630kai/syougen/shinzato-rituko/ [Accessed 9 June 2014].

Soh, S., 2008. *The comfort women: sexual violence and postcolonial memory in Korea and Japan*. Chicago: University of Chicago Press.

Szczepanska, K., 2014. *The politics of war memory in Japan: progressive civil society groups and contestation of memory of the Asia-Pacific War*. London: Routledge.

Tanji, M., 2006. *Myth, protest and struggle in Okinawa*. London: Routledge.

Yonetani, J., 2000. On the battlefield of Mabuni: struggles over peace and the past in contemporary Okinawa. *East Asian History*, 20, 145–168.

Yonetani, J., 2001. Playing base politics in a global strategic theatre: Futenma relocation, the G-8, summit, and Okinawa. *Critical Asian Studies*, 33 (1), 70–95.

From Tokyo to The Hague: war crime tribunals and (shifting?) memory politics in Japan

KERSTIN LUKNER

Abstract: While studies on Japanese memory politics have taken up, for example, Diet members' visits to Yasukuni Shrine and depictions of Japan's wartime conduct in school textbooks, few scholars have examined the country's membership in the International Criminal Court (ICC). However, the ICC is an intriguing case for analysis, as the court that prosecutes individuals for war crimes, crimes against humanity, genocide and the crime of aggression (i.e. crimes against peace) is commonly portrayed as the successor of the Nuremberg and Tokyo War Crime Tribunals. Despite discussions in Japan revealing a rather negative stance towards the Tokyo Tribunal and its rulings, often dubbed 'victor's justice', the government has overall appeared supportive of the creation of the ICC and Japan eventually became a member in 2007. Against this backdrop, this article explores whether Tokyo's ICC membership can be regarded an exception to Japan's generally rather defensive memory politics and if so why this is the case. Based on an analysis of Diet debates, an investigation of the legal changes made in the context of Japan's ICC accession as well as an examination of the government's attitude towards current wartime compensation charges against Japanese companies, the article demonstrates that ICC membership is not an outlier, but it rather confirms Japan's approach to memory politics seen in other areas.

Introduction

Historical issues loom large in Japan's foreign relations with its Asian neighbours and are also contested in Japan's domestic political arena. Well-known examples are the controversies relating to Diet members' visits to Yasukuni Shrine, the (non-) compensation of former sex-slaves ('comfort women') and depictions in school textbooks trivializing the crimes committed by imperial Japan. In a more recent case, current Prime Minister Abe Shinzō expressed his doubts about Japan's military intervention during the Second World War qualifying as aggression. Besides stirring anger in Beijing and Seoul, this also led to criticism in the Japanese Diet (Hyun-ki and Kim, 9 May 2013), illustrating how Japanese politicians are frequently at odds with each other about how to reflect and act upon their country's contested past (Hein 2010, pp. 151–153; Kristof 1995, Sakaki 2012). In this context, Japan's accession to the International Criminal Court (ICC) is an interesting case for examination; the Court is often portrayed as the successor of the Nuremberg and Tokyo War Crimes Tribunals due to its prosecution of core international crimes, i.e. war crimes, genocide, crimes against humanity and the crime of aggression. Three features of the case are striking: first, while negative views of the Tokyo Tribunal and the 'victor's justice' thereby established dominate, Japan has overall appeared supportive of the creation of the ICC in 2002 and became a member in 2007. Second, the Lower and Upper Houses of Japan's national Diet were not divided on the question of membership, but rather voted unanimously in favour of Japan's accession to the ICC. Third, Japan's decision to join the Court has provoked no reaction worth mentioning among its history-sensitive neighbours, especially China and South Korea. Likewise, it has attracted remarkably little attention among the scholars of historical memory.

Against this backdrop, the article sheds light on Tokyo's ICC membership in the context of Japan's memory politics. Specifically, it explores whether Japan's accession to the ICC hints at a partial shift in the state's assessment of the Tokyo Tribunal's contested historical legacy. This question has been left largely unaddressed by legal scholars who have produced most of the literature on Japan's ICC membership thus far (e.g. Arai et al. 2008, pp. 359–383; Higashizawa 2007, pp. 298–317; Kō 2007, pp. 37–42; Masaki 2008, pp. 409–426; Niikura 2007, pp. 25–30). Based on an analysis of various written sources, including scripts of Diet debates, as well as insights gained from interviews with policymakers, bureaucrats and academics working in the field, this article holds that Tokyo's decision to accede to the ICC cannot be regarded as an exception to Japan's memory politics seen in other areas. Developing this argument in more detail, the article is structured as follows: the next section defines political memory and describes the way the International Military Tribunal for the Far East (IMTFE), the 1946 to 1948 major war crimes tribunal conducted in Tokyo, is remembered in mainstream Japanese politics but also contested up to this day. Section three illustrates politicians' evaluation of the ICC in the context of their rather negative remembrance of the IMTFE. It also highlights the reasons for Japan's decision to join the ICC despite misgivings. The fourth section examines the legal adjustment process that Japan underwent when joining ICC, evaluating the measures taken in the context of its IMTFE experience. In the fifth section, the article scrutinizes the government's attitude towards compensation charges that former war time slave labourers have recently put forth against Japanese companies in South Korean and Chinese courts, assessing whether Tokyo's ICC membership has led to a more conciliatory position towards those Asian victims of Japanese war time aggression who were largely ignored during the IMTFE proceedings. In the final section, the article summarizes the main findings, holding that Japan's accession to the ICC does not point to any fundamental change in its memory politics relating to criminal justice and punishment.

The analysis offers three key research findings. First, Japanese political debates treat the IMTFE experience and the formation of the ICC as disconnected. In Japan, there is no positive 'IMTFE legacy' that triggered support for the first permanent international criminal court in history. Any connections established between the two are confined to the observation that the founders of the ICC 'rightly' avoided the many flaws that had plagued its Japanese 'predecessor.' This view as well as an emphasis on the advantages of joining the organization have facilitated Japan's accession to the ICC. Second, the legal changes in Japan's penal code implemented in the context of its ICC membership – in order to enable Japan to conduct criminal proceedings with regards to war crimes, genocide, crimes against humanity and the crime of aggression on its own[1] – were kept to a minimum, which stands in stark contrast to Germany's much more comprehensive take on legal adjustments. By pursuing a minimalist as opposed to Berlin's maximalist approach, Tokyo appears not to acknowledge the severity of the term 'core international crimes'. This suggests an insufficient reflection on the very substance of the ICC's four core crime categories, which may be related to Japan's own lack of facing up to its troubling past. Third, despite Tokyo's support for the ICC, the government is dismissive towards claims currently under consideration in South Korean and Chinese national courts, where individuals are suing Japanese companies for wartime forced labour compensation. The government advises Japanese companies against following court orders – if issued – to pay compensation, fearing that this may undermine the official bilaterally negotiated post-Second World War settlements on compensation and reparation. While this position seems reasonable in the strict terms of legality, it does not reflect the moral ideals embodied by the ICC's work, such as promoting accountability for serious (past) wrongdoings.

IMTFE and the politics of memory in Japan

Different individuals and communities remember and forget the past and its traumatic events, such as wars or war crime tribunals, in various ways. At the state level, the manner in which the past is officially remembered, i.e. the kind of memory that is fostered, is crucially relevant for informing the way a state and its representatives act in the present. Memory describes 'the process or faculty whereby events or impressions from the past are recollected and preserved' (Bell 2006, p. 2). Thus, memory does not exist objectively, but is rather socially constructed through discursive interaction. The term 'memory politics' highlights political actors as agents in this process of creating memory and characterizes 'efforts by political elites, their supporters, and their opponents to construct meanings of the past and propagate them [...] widely or impose them on other members of society' (Lebow 2006, p. 13).[2] While such moves frequently result in the production of competing images of the past and contested memories within the political arena and beyond, state authorities can make use of several means to shape the *official* historical narrative. Relating to wartime experience, these can include rhetoric, commemoration, education, compensation as well as criminal justice and punishment (Berger 2012, p. 12). Needless to say, the official version of history that is thus generated has an important impact on the shaping of the collective memory of a nation, i.e. 'widely shared perceptions of the past' at the societal level (Bell 2006, p. 2). Yet, different societal groups within a state may call this mainstream historical interpretation into question. For example, the prevalent view that the IMTFE was a highly unfair trial and reflective of 'victor's justice' is certainly not shared by all Japanese nor by all members of the international community. In today's globalized world, state authorities are far from able to monopolize one single historical storyline, but the official – and often dominant – historical narrative has still far-reaching political implications. This is because shared understandings of the past, as created and reflected by the official historical narrative, produce or confirm specific norms, values, and commitments (Lebow 2006, p. 3), all of which serve as building blocks for the identity of nations. Moreover, the particular way in which historical memory is framed, or gradually reframed, generates a certain set of policy-lessons for political decision-makers; it informs political judgement and action. For this reason, memory scholars emphasize the integral link between perceptions of the past and the shaping of current politics (Lebow 2006 p. 2).[3] It is this aspect that is of crucial importance to the study at hand.

This article addresses Japan's memory politics relating to the country's highly controversial post-Second World War criminal justice and punishment experience, and also briefly deals with reparation issues. As has been laid out before, it asks if Japan's ICC membership is reflective of any change in the way the state avows to its own war crimes tribunal, i.e. the IMTFE. If this is the case, could this be indicative of an ideational shift relating to the assessment of war crime tribunals within the country's governing elite? If not, how is the ICC membership brought in line with Tokyo's critical stance towards the IMTFE? Before scrutinizing the nature of the connection made between the two courts in current Japanese politics, the next section outlines Japan's politics of memory[4] on the IMTFE. It first briefly sketches the criticism commonly raised about the trial and then shows how the Japanese government has reflected on the IMTFE's historical legacy thus far.

The United States, which took the lead in organizing and conducting the IMTFE, pursued several educative purposes with the trial, including the demilitarization and democratization of nationalist Japan. Not only were major

Japanese war criminals to be brought to justice, but also their wrongdoings needed to be acknowledged by the Japanese people (Futamura 2008, p. 56). Moreover, the IMTFE was meant to advance and authorize a specific account of the war as well as war responsibility, laying the basis for a particular historical narrative to be accepted by the Japanese (Futamura 2008, p. 58). The Tribunal's jurisdiction covered three categories of crimes, namely crimes against peace (class A), conventional war crimes (class B) and crimes against humanity (class C). At the end of the proceedings, all 25 political and military leaders of wartime Japan on trial in Tokyo were found guilty[5] with seven receiving a death sentence (Futamura 2008, p. 55). In addition to the major war crimes tribunal in Tokyo, various trials against suspects of class B and class C crimes were conducted all over Asia (Berger 2012, pp. 144–145).

However, various aspects of the IMTFE drew extensive criticism both in Japan and abroad.[6] First, the prosecution's most serious charge, according to which the leaders of imperial Japan had engaged in a conspiracy to wage a war of aggression and were thus punishable for having committed crimes against peace, was called into question. In international law, such a crime category had not existed at the time of the war,[7] meaning that the major Japanese defendants (who were later convicted as class A war criminals) were charged on an ex-post facto law basis. Second, the emperor, who was the official head of state during the war, was not indicted but granted immunity due to political considerations of the US occupation authorities. Third, the trial itself was plagued by numerous procedural flaws and conducted in a surprisingly careless manner. For example, the chief prosecutor mishandled evidence and the defence team was restricted in its access to resources. Moreover, the whole trial rested upon the Anglo-American legal system unfamiliar to the Japanese. Fourth, under its Western (or rather US) leadership, the IMTFE concentrated on the acts of war between Japan and the US as well as its Western allies, while largely ignoring the harm inflicted on Japan's Asian neighbours. For instance, the suffering of sex slaves and victims of bacteriological experiments were not addressed during the proceedings. Fifth (and partly following from these flaws), there was no unanimous judgment when the final verdict was proclaimed, with two of the eleven international judges dissenting. Five wrote separate opinions (Futamura 2008, p. 54).[8] This expression of disagreement within the bench foreshadowed the high level of contestation that would accompany all later assessments of the IMTFE experience. Indian Justice Radhabinod Pal's extensive dissent became the most well-known, holding that the IMTFE was based on ex-post facto legislation and evidence of defendants' conspiracy to wage a war of aggression was inconclusive. Pal also raised questions about the war crimes committed by the US and its allies. On the one hand, this point resonated well with many ordinary Japanese, who had first-hand experience of the war and saw themselves as victims of terrible crimes – especially due to the dropping of atomic bombs on Hiroshima and Nagasaki (Tanaka 2006). On the other hand, in the immediate post-war era, various Japanese legal scholars viewed the trial and its verdict as largely legitimate (Osten 2003, p. 117). In short, the IMTFE and its ruling were contested within (and also outside) Japan right from the start. Yet, at the official state level, the Japanese government accepted the IMTFE's controversial verdict by signing the San Francisco Peace Treaty in 1951 to regain sovereignty one year later – but it quite clearly also lacked alternatives.

The Tokyo Trial's view of history and wartime memory it sought to generate, i.e. that Japan had been guilty of planning and conducting a war of aggression in Asia, hardly gained ground in the mainstream Japanese perception of the war. Rather, the IMTFE and its ruling came to be seen as 'victor's justice'. Thus, around the time the occupation ended, many Japanese were already in favour of pardoning their imprisoned fellow countrymen. Such demands were somewhat met by the US occupation authorities as early as 1950, partly because of a readjustment in US strategic calculations concerning Japan due to intensifying Cold War tensions. Prison sentences were reduced or in some cases convicted criminals even received parole (Berger 2012, p. 146). After Japan regained sovereignty in 1952, Tokyo made no effort to initiate its own war crime tribunal to domestically deal with the perpetrators of wartime aggression and atrocities (Lind 2008, p. 35). Rather it engaged in a campaign to have all ongoing trials relating to class B and C criminals stopped. This government stance was backed by a popular movement calling for the release of all Japanese war criminals. Already in 1953, it had collected more than 15 million signatures (Buruma 2009, p. 169). Full success was eventually achieved in 1958 when all Japanese war criminals were released and subsequently politically rehabilitated (Tanaka 2006). Since former prisoners had not been charged under Japanese law, but evidently under some dubious international law, they were even entitled to receive back salaries and pensions (Lind 2008, p. 35) – a situation clearly indicating that the verdicts of the IMTFE and the many other tribunals relating to class B and class C crimes were 'reversed entirely' in the end (Berger 2012, p. 146). On balance, it seems that the Tribunal did not generate the educational effect originally envisioned by the US. It was unable to instil a particular view of history, i.e. one along the dichotomy of Japanese aggressor versus foreign victims, and way of remembering the war in the Japanese people.

Undermining the IMTFE's original aim, several politicians who had been deeply enmeshed in wartime politics were able to successfully re-enter the domestic political arena in the 1950s, primarily because their political experience was needed to rebuild the country. Two of them are particularly noteworthy: first, Shigemitsu Mamoru, who acted as foreign minister and later on minister for Greater East Asia in the early 1940s and was convicted as a class A war criminal by the IMTFE, became the country's foreign minister in 1954. He later also represented Japan at its first United Nations plenary session after it had joined the organization in 1956 (Togo 2008, p. 60). Furthermore, Kishi Nobusuke, a high-ranking official in Manchuria in the 1930s and munitions minister in the early 1940s, who was arrested as a class A war criminal but never put on trial after the war, became Japan's prime minister in 1957 (Berger 2012, p. 146). It goes without saying that such conservative politicians did not promote a self-critical historical narrative (Berger 2009, p. 24); nor did they develop any appreciation for the IMTFE which, after all, aimed at assigning accountability to those deemed responsible for Japan's conduct during the war.[9] Instead, after Japan's regaining sovereignty, politicians such as Kishi engaged in activities to ensure that all Japanese war criminals would eventually be released from prison (Lind 2008, p. 35). Symptomatic of his attitude towards the IMTFE was the move to invite Pal, the Indian IMTFE justice who strongly disagreed with the final verdict, to Japan several times to grant him honours. The dismissive attitude towards the Tokyo Trial, which is reflected in such deeds of political symbolism and importance, has been continuing to this day — at least when it comes to conservative politicians such as representatives of the ruling LDP (Liberal Democratic Party). For example, when Kishi's grandson, current Prime Minister Abe Shinzō, visited India during his first term in office (2006–2007) he paid homage to Pal in a speech delivered to the Indian parliament in his capacity as head of the Japanese government (Onishi 2007). Prime Minister Abe, who is well known for his nationalist thinking, strongly indicated disapproval of the IMTFE verdict in his speech, yet stopped short of calling it outright into question. His criticism aimed at the IMTFE is in line with assessments put forward by rightists ever since the beginning of the 1990s, claiming that the Tokyo Tribunal and its judgement embody a 'self-negating historical view' (*tōkyō saiban jigyaku shikan*) (Togo 2010, p. 30). In fact, one of Abe's major political-ideological goals is to 'correct' the 'masochistic view of history' (*jigyaku shikan*) as it was presumably established by the IMTFE among others. His perception is certainly not shared by most Japanese who continue to be critical of the IMTFE, on the one hand, but do not endorse those who were convicted, on the other. Still, Abe's ambitions illustrate how the historical memory of the war and the subsequent war crimes tribunal both remain sites of contention to this day.

In short, while formally respecting the IMTFE judgement due to foreign pressure, Japanese political and collective memory on post-Second World War criminal justice concentrates on the weaknesses of the Tokyo Tribunal ('victor's justice'), thus working towards the de-legitimization of its outcome, at least at an informal level. Of course, the IMTFE's various flaws can be rightly pointed out and criticized. At the same time, such a narrow focus seems to serve the political purpose of diverting attention away from questions of key importance, i.e. whether those accused in Tokyo were guilty of having committed grave crimes or not. In Japan, the paradox inherent in the dominant thinking on the IMTFE is that the Trial's flaws are vividly remembered whereas many of the heinous crimes prosecuted by the Court are forgotten (Cohen 2003, p. 51). Yet, solely putting the focus on the shortcomings of the Tribunal prevents many Japanese from acknowledging that the Tribunal intended to establish criminal accountability for war crimes and other mass atrocities, and thus put an end to what the ICC calls a 'culture of impunity', for one of the first times in history. Thus, despite all the arguments relating to the IMTFE's shortcomings, one legal scholar rightly holds that one 'must not lose sight of the fact that new international law has grown out of the controversial, indeed sometimes questionable, origins [...] in Tokyo' (e.g. Simma 1999, p. 82). For instance, today the legal confrontation with past injustices has become an important part of many transitional justice processes, also in Asia (Jeffery and Kim 2014, p. 25), and it is the core work of the ICC. Yet, when looking at the politics of memory relating to the Tokyo Tribunal in Japan at large — formal acceptance and informal rejection — it is doubtful if the establishment of such a positive relation between the IMTFE experience and the development of international (criminal) law is possible in the mind of Japanese political decision-makers. In more concrete terms, (how) have perceptions of the IMTFE shaped the government's attitude towards the ICC? When it comes to creating a new international institution to punish war crimes and related atrocities, what were the policy-lessons to be drawn from Japan's own particular way of remembering its encounter with the IMTFE? Certainly, they might deviate from those drawn by the nations that initiated the Tokyo Tribunal and which might remember its legacy quite differently, i.e. in a more positive light. Equally important, what was Tokyo's main rationale for eventually acceding to the ICC in 2007?

The path from Tokyo to The Hague

Historical, political and legal considerations

Some scholars argue that memory has considerably influenced the shaping of international norms, values and institutions. For example, on the ICC one of them notes, the '[...] Court [...] [was] generated by the lessons of the Holocaust and World War II—and by the Tokyo and Nuremberg Tribunals' (Langenbacher 2010, p. 19). Yet, if we scrutinize and compare state reactions to the idea of setting up novel international institutions that derive from historical experience to some extent, we cannot expect to discover only one uniform lesson that all states have learned by looking back to and reflecting on the past, as the Japanese reaction to the founding of the ICC subsequently illustrates. At first sight, the bare facts suggest Tokyo was supportive of the ICC project, but looking at Japan's stance in more detail, it becomes clear that the country was hesitant in its policy on the ICC throughout the establishment and accession process. In fact, when negotiations on the creation of an international criminal court started at the United Nations shortly after the end of the Cold War, several observers, such as those from non-governmental human rights organizations, were sceptical about Japan's commitment to the idea of setting up such an institution (Pace 2006, p. 1). It does not seem far-fetched to partly attribute this scepticism to

Tokyo's specific historical understanding of the IMTFE encounter. Yet, while Japan might not have been the most outspoken proponent of a future ICC, it became actively involved in the negotiation process, e.g. jointly with Germany demanding the recognition of the crime of aggression as a core international crime. After all, crimes against peace – i.e. the crime of aggression – had been the main charge in Tokyo as well as in Nuremberg (Schabas 2004, p. 32). Also, when consultations on a founding treaty for the ICC reached an impasse at the final stage of international negotiations in 1998 due to diverging views on the specific scope of its work, the leader of the Japanese delegation team, Owada Hisashi,[10] showed himself committed to finding compromise (Owada and Shibahara 1999) and thus to saving the ICC project. In the end, Japan voted in favour of adopting the treaty on the establishment of the ICC,[11] but it neither signed nor ratified the so-called Rome Statute to support its coming into effect afterwards for various reasons, which are explained in the subsequent sections.[12] Still, the sixty signatures that were necessary for the treaty to enter into force were accumulated by 2002, kicking off the operation of the ICC in the same year. This important event put Japan under pressure to more clearly indicate its stance on the prospects of a future ICC membership, but the government cautiously kept reiterating the following basic position: while Tokyo was generally supportive of the ICC, it first needed to examine the legal requirements that would follow from Japan's ICC membership and secondly deal with domestic law adjustments that might become necessary.[13] However, the legal review and adjustment process did not start until 2006,[14] and Japan could not avoid giving the impression of being hesitant to join the ICC for other than legal reasons.

On closer examination it becomes clear that the country indeed had to overcome diverse obstacles before joining the ICC, including important legal issues that arose due to the many constraints in its defence policy. For instance, as a pacifist country that was severely restricted in its military capabilities due to Article 9 of its constitution (the so-called 'peace clause'), Japan had not yet implemented the Geneva Conventions and their Protocols when the ICC started operating in 2002. Yet, those core treaties of international humanitarian law regulate the conduct during armed conflict and are meant to prevent the occurrence of war crimes (which constitute one of the ICC's core crime categories). In the context of Japan's possible ICC membership, the fact that the country was not yet officially bound by the Geneva Conventions and its Protocols, at least in legal terms, came to be seen as problematic. For example, Japan lacked a legal basis to punish the perpetrators of war crimes. This situation only changed in 2003 and was mostly the result of modified threat perceptions after the 9/11 terrorist attacks on the US, prompting the implementation of emergency legislation (*yūji hōsei*) including all parts of the Geneva Conventions in Japan (Lukner 2007, pp. 98–100). Furthermore, given the stark US hostility toward the ICC due to sovereignty concerns, Japanese decision-makers had to deal with the question of how Washington, its only alliance partner and sole security guarantor, would react to a Japanese ICC membership. The US pursued various obstructionist policies toward the ICC and its active supporters in the first part of the 2000s, but Washington weakened its opposition before the end of the second Bush administration, which lasted until early 2009 (Lukner 2012, p. 101). Both developments certainly laid some important ground for Japan's willingness to seriously consider its accession to the ICC.

In addition to the initial legal and security concerns just described, Japan's reluctance to join the Court also appeared connected to the long shadow of its own War Crimes Tribunal experience. First, some domestic observers, such as those of the Japanese right, seem to have feared that an ICC membership could result in a renewed indictment of Japanese war crimes (Goold 2002), including questions about the responsibility of the Japanese emperor.[15] While such discussions appear to have brought up bad memories relating to the IMTFE within right-wing political circles, the ICC is in fact not allowed to deal with crimes that happened before its creation in 2002. Second, other observers speculated whether the government initially backed off from joining the Court in order not to trigger a domestic debate on war crimes and atrocities committed by imperial Japan (Lukner 2007, p. 96), as many of them had just become punishable acts under international criminal law. Possibly, this could have led to a shift in the debates' focus away from emphasizing the IMTFE's procedural weaknesses towards a closer examination of the very substance of the crimes it had been concerned with, at least in the less controversial B and C categories. Third, at the level of the country's bureaucracy, representatives of the Ministry of Justice seemed to have been afraid that an active Japanese support for the ICC could be equated with an explicit ex-post approval of the IMTFE (Osten 2003, p. 182), and this was an impression Japan wanted to avoid.

How was Japan to deal with such controversial issues rooted in history when it finally acceded to the ICC in 2007? Put simply, politicians, decision-makers and government representatives stressed that the law represented by the ICC was clearly enhanced when compared with that represented by the IMTFE. In the light of the ICC's founding in 2002, Tōyama Kiyohiko of the New Kōmeitō, a party that had clearly positioned itself in favour of Japan's ICC membership before it became LDP policy-line a few years later, argued that the ICC judged over 'inhumane acts, irrespective of the winners and losers of the war', and this fact – and we might add difference to the IMTFE – was 'very important'.[16] Similarly, former Justice Minister Moriyama Mayumi (2001–2003) of the LDP, who happened to work at the IMTFE as a student translator and had therefore been able to gain first-hand insights into its proceedings, underlined just how crucial this legal improvement was from the Japanese perspective.[17] In her view, which seems reflective of the general Japanese sentiment, justice gets impaired when the winners of a conflict sit in judgement over those who were defeated. However, the ICC would sit in judgement on crimes committed by the losers as well as winners of wars in a neutral fashion (Moriyama 2007, p. 6). Upon the Diet's decision to support Japan's accession to the ICC in April 2007, then Foreign Minister Asō Tarō likewise compared the IMTFE with the ICC, expressing criticism of the former while stressing the improvements with regard to the latter. In the Diet he argued,

> Japan is not in a position to object to the judgment of the International Military Tribunal for the Far East in state-to-state relations, but with regards to the same Tribunal I recognize several controversies relating to various legal aspects such as the contradiction with the prohibition on punishment on the basis of ex-post facto law. The ICC [...] is based on the general principles of criminal law such as non-retroactivity and no punishment without law to start with [...]. Thus, I think that [the ICC] serves the improvement of the rule of law in the international community.[18]

With their praise about legal improvements, politicians such as Tōyama, Moriyama and Asō were denoting the character of the IMTFE at the same time. Interestingly, representatives of other parties than the LDP and New Kōmeitō, the main ruling parties since the late 1990s, have not voiced a more positive assessment of the relation between the IMTFE and the ICC in Diet debates. The idea that 'world history' had been written in Tokyo or the notion that the proceedings 'had significant influence on the development of international law' are absent in Diet deliberations.[19] Critical-to-negative sentiments towards the IMTFE were also reflected in some newspaper reporting. For instance, after lawmakers had decided positively on Japan's ICC membership, the conservative newspaper *Nihon Keizai Shimbun* (1 July 2007) suggested that Japan, having experienced an ex-post facto war crimes tribunal, should critically check the ICC in order to make sure its verdicts were fair and free from any notions of revenge – and thus different from the IMTFE, the subtext seems to suggest. If we compare both courts, i.e. the IMTFE and the ICC, it becomes clear that the latter actually operates on a very different legal basis. For example, it can only initiate criminal proceedings on its own after a stringent evaluation by a pre-trial chamber, consisting of several judges; it can only investigate crimes that were committed after the Rome Statute came into effect; and it can solely prosecute crimes that were either committed by nationals of ICC member states or committed on their territory. These and other specifications in the Rome Statute are meant to ensure the due process of law.[20]

Why become an ICC member?

Naturally, within the general debate on Japan's ICC membership, contested memory relating to the IMTFE was not always the predominant theme. Rather, different actors at the national as well as international level arguing in favour of Japan's accession to the ICC addressed various other points. This situation indicates yet another layer of contestation in the debate. For instance, human rights advocates such as Amnesty International (AI), and its Japan division in particular, started to campaign for Japan's accession to the ICC soon after the adoption of the Rome Statute in 1998. In fact, as a human rights organization, AI has taken this approach with regards to all nations worldwide, asking for their active participation in the system of international (criminal) justice (AI 2006). AI's goal is to ensure the deterrence of atrocities and thus to avoid the occurrence of grave human rights abuses. The Japan Federation of Bar Association (JFBA, *nihon bengoshi rengōkai*) was initially more reluctant to urge the Japanese government to pursue active participation in the ICC project, partly due to the wide-ranging legal implications of the membership,[21] specifically in the field of security-related laws (as was mentioned above). However, after the 9/11 terrorist attacks on the US, JFBA changed its position. It came to view Japan's full support for the international penal machinery to prosecute core crimes, i.e. ICC membership, as a key alternative to the government's approach of deepening and broadening Japan's military commitments to the international war on terrorism (JFBA 2002). What JFBA wanted to see was Tokyo's holding up the rule of law in international politics rather than the rule of force. Individuals from both organizations, AI and JFBA, also engaged in the Japanese Network for the ICC (JNICC; *kokusai keiji saibanjo nihon nettowāku*). This group of lawyers, human rights activists and students, who believed in the ideals embodied in the Rome Statute and lobbied for Japan's early accession to the ICC, began to raise public and political awareness in 1997. Its activities included the organization of public seminars and study group sessions for Diet members (JNICC 2007).

At the international level, the European Union (EU) was particularly dedicated to supporting the expansion of the ICC membership in order to decrease impunity worldwide. To this end, it actively campaigned in Japan, initiating visits of high-ranking EU delegations to Tokyo in 2002 and 2004. These démarches consisted of ICC-experts from various EU member states as well as representatives from EU institutions such as the Commission, and in 2004 also included officials from the ICC (e.g. from the Prosecutor's Office), all of whom held discussions with Japanese government representatives, bureaucrats, Diet members, academics as well as the public (MOFA 2002, 2004). While the EU generally engages in political dialogue with states that have not become ICC members yet, Japan seems to have been viewed as a key target country in Asia as indicated by the high-level composition of delegations. The EU regards Japan as 'playing a major role in the international system' (Wellenstein 2004) and its support for the ICC was thus seen as vitally important. It is furthermore worth mentioning that Japan's accession to the ICC was to bring about a significant decrease in financial contributions to the Court for the various EU members. While AI, JFBA, JNICC, the EU and others worked to put pressure on Japan with their own particular agendas in mind, what were the Japanese government's main incentives to decide pro ICC membership despite Japan's rather negative historical memory relating to the IMTFE?

Government publications, especially those by the Japanese Ministry of Foreign Affairs (*gaimushō*) or journal articles by its bureaucrats, highlight how Japan's ICC membership emphasizes its position as a major contributor to international cooperation. First, Japan's ICC membership reflects the country's unwillingness to accept impunity for core international crimes, underlying its determination to tighten the grip on the perpetrators of such crimes. Second, accession is seen as a contribution to the geographic coverage of the ICC, increasing the number of Asian members. Third, through membership, Japan is able to proactively take part in the creation and development of international law, such as during the Rome Statute's review conference on the crime of aggression in 2012, thereby contributing to norm-building in the fields of international humanitarian and criminal law. Fourth, as an ICC member Japan is able to place its own personnel within the organization (Gaimushō 2012) and thus have Japanese values reflected and Japanese thinking better understood there (Okazaki 2007, p. 50). Fifth, as an ICC member Japan would substantially contribute to the operation of the Court through taking over the largest share of budget allocations (Gaimushō 2012). All this is said to reflect how Japan is a key pillar of the international community when it comes to taking over those duties and responsibilities connected with international cooperation (Noguchi 2006, p. 246). Thus, through joining the ICC, Japan tries to portray itself as a responsible member of the international community, as a civilized country governed by the rule-of-law; one clearly belonging to the group of advanced countries. Its membership is to demonstrate Japan's desire to hold up and abide by novel international criminal law. Its active ICC support also becomes visible through its annual financial contributions to the Court, which are the largest among all member states, and the number of personnel it sends out to work at the institution. This overtly positive image of law-abiding Japan is in stark contrast to the one constructed by the IMTFE of imperial Japan committing heinous crimes and fighting an unlawful and aggressive war. Therefore, for Japan its accession to the ICC was an opportunity to re-stress its post-Second World War and post-IMTFE identity as a peaceful and law-abiding member of the international community; one that would not accept the occurrence of atrocities and would support a permanent war crimes tribunal that works in a neutral fashion. Japan's policy can be seen as an attempt to supplant the country's image as created by the IMTFE ruling several decades ago.

In sum, Japan's eventual commitment to the ICC does not reveal a departure from its generally critical stance towards the Tokyo Tribunal. Instead, Diet debates show that support for the ICC was based on the Court's very different legal nature and the perception that it would meet much higher levels of fairness and universality when compared with the IMTFE. These arguments strongly suggest that lawmakers did not see any IMTFE legacy embodied in the ICC and no positive connection between the two. Instead, any link would be restricted to the simple fact that the founders of the ICC rightly avoided many of the flaws plaguing the Tokyo Tribunal. This also explains how Japan's policy choice to accede to the ICC could be legitimized against the backdrop of a highly contested historical experience, the perception of which did not need to be altered. When Japan finally joined the Court in 2007, it seized the opportunity to affirm its post-Second World War identity as a peaceful, civilized country, as a rule-of-law state and as an important member of the international community. This also explains how the first Abe government could do both in 2007: honour Justice Pal, on the one hand, and carry out Japan's accession to the ICC, on the other.

(Non-) Adjustment of the Japanese penal code

The ICC is a court that operates on the basis of complementarity, meaning that it only takes charge of criminal proceedings if member states are unable or unwilling to investigate and prosecute core international crimes themselves.[22] As primary responsibility for the prosecution of war crimes, genocide, crimes against humanity, and the crime of aggression lies with the Court's member states, each of them has to consider and decide how exactly to organize the national implementation of the Rome Statute. This is left at their discretion. Interestingly, Germany and Japan, the two countries that share the experience of being the defendants in major international war crimes tribunals right after the end of the Second World War, chose very different paths when it came to incorporating the punishment of ICC crimes into national legislation. While Germany adopted a maximalist position, adding a novel and comprehensive body of international criminal law to its penal code, Japan opted for a minimalist approach, resulting in only minor changes to the existing criminal code. This section analyses the major reasons for Japan to take such a minimalist stance, shedding light on bureaucratic positions, remaining legal problems, and the influence of Japan's own IMTFE experience on that decision.

Prior to officially becoming an ICC member, Tokyo had to identify and adjust the law as deemed necessary in the given context. For Japan, this is standard accession procedure.[23] However, in the case of the ICC the question of precisely how to adjust domestic law provisions in accordance with the requirements of the Rome Statute evolved into a rather contentious issue. Initially, at least, the bureaucrats located in the International Legal Affairs Bureau of the Ministry of Foreign Affairs seemed to have favoured the implementation of new substantive law (Meierhenrich and Ko 2009, p. 19), i.e. legal provisions that define crimes and their punishment. In official Diet debates, Foreign Ministry representatives also considered this particular option (Arai *et al.* 2008, p. 367). That is to say, the pro-ICC Foreign Ministry officials in particular thought it necessary to either have the existing penal code extensively revised or – just like Germany – an additional penal code for the prosecution of core international crimes enacted in order to enable Japan to fully punish all ICC core crimes in accordance with the Rome Statute (Saiki 2002, p. 11). However, as Japan's criminal law system is 'finely calibrated, and treated as such' (Meierhenrich and Ko 2009, p. 12), their idea of introducing new principles and crimes to Japan's criminal code was met with little enthusiasm. Representatives of the Ministry of Justice in particular rejected the idea of having to formulate and introduce new laws to Japan's penal system.[24] Eventually, the controversy was solved by bureaucrats agreeing that most ICC crimes could be punished under Japan's penal code as domestic crimes (Meierhenrich and Ko 2009, p. 13), and no further changes needed to be implemented. In 2007, after nine years of allegedly studying the scope and complexity of the necessary adjustments at the level of domestic law, this minimalist solution became the official government position.

While some commentators appreciate the minimalist approach as pragmatic, asserting that it avoided an even longer delay in Japan's accession to the ICC (e.g. Niikura 2007, p. 28), it remains highly controversial. This is because by applying such an approach, the complexity of ICC core crimes and the related elements of these crimes has not been transferred to and is now nowhere reflected in the Japanese penal code. After all, the primary purpose of the existing penal code is to tackle the prosecution of ordinary crimes, not to deal with the 'most serious crimes of concern to the international community as a whole'.[25] Consequently, sceptics question whether large-scale atrocities can be *adequately* dealt with under Japanese criminal law (Inazumi 2008, pp. 423–24). To give a particular example, under current Japanese law, 'extermination' as a crime against humanity, or genocide, would have to be treated as 'multiple homicides' resulting in a large number of fatalities (Meierhenrich and Ko 2009, pp. 13–14, 24). Critics argue that the degree of injustice as embodied in the four core international crimes, i.e. genocide, crimes against humanity, war crimes and the crime of aggression, is not sufficiently covered by Japan's domestic criminal code and that its application simply appears inappropriate for such grave offenses.[26] Moreover, Japan's penal code does not fully address several legal concepts that are part of the Rome Statute, such as the non-applicability of the statute of limitations, the notion of command responsibility or the idea that conspiracy to commit atrocities constitutes a punishable crime (Inazumi 2008, pp. 430–432; Meierhenrich and Ko 2009: 13 ff.), consequently highlighting the profound problems in Japan's minimalist approach from the perspective of complementarity. This situation is particularly noteworthy since the government is usually eager to ensure that there is no gap between domestic law provisions and international obligations (Inazumi 2008, p. 421). However, even if highly unlikely, in the case a Japanese citizen committed one of the crimes described in the Rome Statute and not covered by Japan's domestic penal code, this person would have to be transferred to ICC to face legal proceedings in The Hague. If such a scenario became real and a Japanese national had to face a war crimes tribunal presided over by a bench of foreign judges, the historical memory of the IMTFE would most certainly be revived. Even in light of such a scenario, changing the language of the country's criminal code did not seem worth the effort. Given Japan's post-war identity as a peace-loving and law-abiding nation, most bureaucrats as well as politicians in Tokyo seemed unable to actually imagine a situation where Japanese nationals could come under suspicion of having committed core international crimes (Masaki 2007, p. 31).[27] Still, in an effort to point to alternative, more comprehensive and perhaps judicially less problematic approaches, legal scholars refer to the case of Germany at times (e.g. Niikura 2007, p. 28).[28] Berlin applied a maximalist position, enacting a whole new Code of Crimes against International Law that extensively defines all four core international crime categories and attempts to ensure their proper punishment in accordance with specifications of the Rome Statute.[29] Despite most members of Japan's political establishment agreeing that the country would probably never have to deal with perpetrators of core international crimes, let alone with ones of Japanese descent, pointing to the weaknesses of the minimalist approach and referring to such alternatives did not completely fall on deaf ears. It is for this reason that — in the context of their supporting the minimalist way to accession — both houses of the national Diet called on the government to ensure that Japan would be able to indict and prosecute all ICC-related crimes in the future (Nakauchi 2007, p. 10). Yet, no further action to amend the penal code has followed so far.

In sum, Japan's decision to apply a minimalist approach, when adjusting its criminal code in accordance with the requirements of the Rome Statute, is based on legal as well as political pragmatism. However, in comparison with more extensive domestic legal adjustment processes that resulted out of other international treaty obligations such as those related to transnational terrorism (Meierhenrich and Ko 2009 pp. 18–19), the Japanese approach towards the ICC turns out to be particularly low-key and indicative of a rather non-committal attitude. Simply put, 'the "minimalist approach" requires minimum effort' only (Inazumi 2008, p. 423). In the context of Japan's critical-to-dismissive stance vis-à-vis the IMTFE, this approach seems also to have been chosen as a way of sidestepping key questions about Japan's own past. For instance, by choosing this course of action, government representatives and lawmakers were largely able to avoid dealing with the historically contested concepts of conspiracy and command responsibility at length, both of which played key roles during the IMTFE proceedings.[30] Had the Japanese created new substantive law and specified all four core international crimes in the penal code, they would have needed to reflect more profoundly about the nature of such crimes. Furthermore, particular episodes of Japan's own conduct during the Second World War might have met their definitions in retrospect, prompting questions about Japan's war guilt. Moreover, adopting a 'maximalist approach' could have further exposed the fact that there is in fact an IMTFE legacy to be found in the ICC — as various observers have been arguing in the context of establishing the latter. Yet, the legal path taken by Japan seemed useful to circumvent extensive discussions on such controversial issues. On the whole, this does not point to change but continuity in Japan's memory politics relating to the IMTFE and appears to substantiate the idea that perceptions of the past are able to influence political decision-making even several decades later. Instead of a willingness to dig into contested history-related issues, discussions on the legal adjustment process rather reveal just how much Japan's post-war national identity as a peaceful, law-abiding country is consolidated: most members of Japan's political establishment could hardly imagine Japanese nationals being involved in committing core international crimes. Calls for a more extensive adjustment of the domestic penal code to address remaining legal problems and complementarity issues can thus primarily be regarded as reflecting the desire to uphold the integrity of the law enshrined in the Rome Statute, and thus to reinforce Japan's image as a rule-of-law state, not allowing for legal loopholes for the perpetrators of core international crimes (who would probably be of other national origin).

From The Hague back to Northeast Asia

Current developments relating to wartime forced labour compensation cases, brought before domestic courts in South Korea and China and aimed against Japanese companies, seem to support the impression that the Japanese government sees little connection between its support for the ICC and the ideals it represents, on the one hand, and its dealing with some of its own contested historical issues, on the other. Courts in South Korea and China have recently started to accept lawsuits by individuals who claim compensation payments for conscripted labour performed in Japanese companies during the Second World War. A Beijing court has accepted a class action suit against two Japanese companies, Mitsubishi Materials as well as Nippon Coke and Engineering, in May 2014 for the first time ever (Yamada 2014). Moreover, two courts in South Korea have already ordered Japanese companies to pay compensation in 2013, but the latter have filed appeals (Martin and Jun 2013). It is noteworthy that the Seoul High Court, dealing with actions against Nippon Steel and Sumitomo Metal, ruled that the corporation had committed 'crimes against humanity by joining the Japanese government in mobilising forced labour for the sake of the war of aggression' (McCurry, 11 July 2013), thus mentioning no less than two of the crime categories in its ruling that constitute core international crimes according to the Rome Statute.[31] While those Japanese companies standing on trial appear to consider paying compensation in case their appeals fail – as they would otherwise run the risk of having their assets in South Korea seized – the national government in Tokyo explicitly warns against such a move, fearing that it might undermine the legitimacy of existing compensation agreements. The individual plaintiffs obviously regard the same arrangements as insufficient, but Tokyo argues that further payments would inflict the 'first hole in wartime issues that have been resolved in the 1965 treaty' on the normalization of diplomatic ties between Japan and South Korea, that also included the final settlement of compensation issues, and therefore could not be tolerated (Martin and Jun 2013).[32] Seen strictly from the perspective of legality, the Japanese government's position might appear reasonable. Nonetheless, it does not reflect the norms embodied in the work of the ICC, among them the endorsement of accountability for serious (past) wrongdoings and the promotion of reconciliation efforts.

While issues of reparation and compensation were not covered by the IMTFE at the time (but by the San Francisco Peace Treaty and other bilateral agreements), it is important to note that they are a key element of the Rome Statute, which does not only include provisions on the founding of the ICC but also on the creation of a Trust Fund for Victims (TFV).[33] This Fund is based on the idea that victims of core international crimes shall have the right to claim reparations before the ICC. The TFV's work comprises two aspects. First, it deals with ICC-backed reparation claims against convicted persons, and second, it organizes general assistance for victims financed by donor contributions.[34] Interestingly, Tokyo has recently decided to contribute a first voluntary payment of approximately €600,000 to the TFV,[35] indicating the government's support for the Rome Statute's inclusive approach, consisting of retributive and reparative elements, when coping with particularly grave crimes. Yet, how are we to interpret this stance in the context of Tokyo firmly rejecting recent compensation claims by former South Korean and Chinese slave labourers against Japanese companies? At the risk of repetition, it seems to indicate that the government sees little conceptual connection between its support for current developments in transitional justice, on the one hand, and its dealing with Japan's historical legacy, on the other. Without adopting such a stance, it would be more difficult for Tokyo to sustain its negative approach toward the IMTFE and current compensation claims.

Conclusion

This article argues that Japan's accession to the ICC in 2007 does not indicate any fundamental change in its official historical narrative or its memory politics relating to the IMTFE for three reasons. First, many international legal scholars see the establishment of the ICC in 2002 as the culmination of an evolutionary process that includes the creation of the post-Second World War Nuremberg and Tokyo Trials as important milestones (e.g. Schabas 2004, chapter 1). By contrast, Japanese politicians see no positive IMTFE legacy in the genesis of the ICC, but tend to view both courts as being disconnected. Given that the 'standard understanding' of the IMTFE up to this day focuses on 'victor's justice' (Totani 2009, p. 2), decision-makers evaluate the ICC positively because it seems free from flaws that plagued the Tokyo War Crimes Tribunal. If any connection between both Courts is established in Japanese debates, it is usually narrowed down to this important distinction. Yet, Japan not only joined the ICC due to its advanced legal nature, but also with the intention of boasting its postwar identity as a responsible and law-abiding member of the international community and distinguishing itself from the IMTFE-induced image as an aggressive outcast. Secondly, the adjustment of Japanese criminal law made in the accession context turned out to be minimal, as bureaucrats and politicians claimed that core international crimes could already be punished under the Japanese penal code. A substantive debate on the very nature of those crimes thus did not evolve among Japanese lawmakers, precluding critical reflections on Japanese wrongdoings during the Second World War and the question whether they would – in retrospect – qualify as core international crimes. Consequently, the negative view of the IMTFE could be sustained despite Japan's ICC membership. Third, Japan's endorsement of the ICC and the TFV does not reflect back on the government's stance on recent reparation demands, brought forth by individual South Korean and Chinese slave labourers and aimed at Japanese companies. Tokyo completely rejects the legality of such claims, holding that they had already been settled in the past. Thus, the government fails to take up normative considerations about the promotion of accountability for (past) atrocities that drive much of the ICC's work. In sum, despite Tokyo's ICC membership, official memory politics relating to criminal justice and punishment in the wake of the Second World War has apparently not changed at all in Japan. Yet, the question as to how exactly the IMTFE's legacy should be interpreted and utilized in the present remains contested to this day.

Acknowledgements

The author would like to thank the three anonymous reviewers, as well as Glenn Hook, Luli von der Does-Ishikawa, Giovanni Bulian, and Alexandra Sakaki for their helpful comments on earlier drafts of this article. She is grateful to Tarina Greyling for her research assistance. The author would also like to thank the Japan Society for the Promotion of Science for generously funding a field trip to Japan in 2008.

Disclosure statement

No potential conflict of interest was reported by the author.

Notes

1. The crime of aggression had not been defined when Japan became an ICC member in 2007 and thus provisions on its punishment did not need to be implemented at the time.
2. Note that Lebow uses the term 'institutional memory' instead of 'politics of memory'.
3. This is a social constructivist line of argument. For more detailed accounts on constructivism and memory see, for example, Lebow (2006).

4. In this paper, the terms 'politics of memory' and 'memory politics' are used interchangeably.
5. Of the 25 defendants, two had already died while in custody and one had been discharged due to mental illness (Futamura 2008, p. 54).
6. The following points of criticism are adopted from Berger (2009, pp. 23–24; Berger 2012, pp. 144–146), who analysed key publications on the subject.
7. The notion of such a crime was first introduced at the Nuremberg Trials and was based on natural law thinking.
8. The judges came from the Australia, Canada, China, France, Great Britain, India, the Netherland, New Zealand, the Philippines, the Soviet Union and the United States.
9. For Kishi, in particular, working against the effects of the IMTFE was an issue of key concern (Bix 2000, p. 612).
10. Owada was also permanent representative of Japan to the United Nations from 1994 to 1998, and has been a judge at the International Court of Justice since 2003.
11. Japan thus deviated from the position of its long-time ally (and IMTFE-initiator), the US.
12. The Statute establishes the four core international crimes, describes the structure and function of the ICC and determines rules for the ICC's jurisdiction.
13. For example, explanations by Justice Minister, Chieko Nōno, and Parliamentary Vice Minister for Foreign Affairs, Itsunori Onodera. 163rd Diet, Justice Committee, House of Representatives, Record of Proceedings, 28 October 2005.
14. Interview by the author with a bureaucrat from Japan's Ministry of Foreign Affairs who was involved in the accession process (Tokyo, 8 September 2008).
15. After emperor Hirohito who ruled Japan during the Second World War died in 1989, his son Akihito took over the throne.
16. Speech of Tōyama Kiyohiko, Foreign Policy and Defence Committee, House of Counsellors, Record of Proceedings, 14 April 2002.
17. Interview by the author with former Justice Minister Moriyama Mayumi (Tokyo, 3 September 2008).
18. Speech of Foreign Minister Tarō Asō, Plenary Session, House of Counsellors, Record of Proceedings, 13 April 2007.
19. These quotes (translation by author) are taken from the website of the 'Memoriam Nuremberg Trials Museum', see www.memorium-nuremberg.de (accessed 25 March 2014).
20. For details see Rome Statute of the International Criminal Court, http://legal.un.org/icc/statute/romefra.htm.
21. Personal conversation with Meiji Gakuin law professor Yasushi Higashizawa (JFBA as well as JNICC member), Tokyo, summer 2008.
22. Rome Statute, Art. 17.
23. Usually, the Japanese government first carries out adjustments to Japan's domestic laws or enacts new laws/regulations before entering into the international treaty that it deems to require such legal changes (Iwasawa 1998, p. 27).
24. Interview with IMTFE-expert and Keio law professor Philipp Osten (Tokyo, 5 September 2008).
25. Rome Statute, Preamble.
26. Interview with Philipp Osten (Tokyo, 5 September 2008).
27. Speech by Foreign Minister Tarō Asō, Plenary Session, House of Representatives, Record of Proceedings, 22 March 2007.
28. For a comparison of both countries' approaches see Suzuki (2008).
29. For the text of the 'Code of Crimes against International Law' see http://www.dw.de/popups/pdf/1109851/code-of-crimes-against-international-lawpdf.pdf (accessed 25 March 2014).

30. With regards to the latter concept, Meierhenrich and Ko (2009, p. 18), for example, argue that Japan's 'palpable distrust of the doctrine of command [...] responsibility harks back, in part, to the treatment of Japanese military commanders before the [IMTFE]'.
31. South Korea is one of the 18 Asian ICC members and joined the Court as early as 2002.
32. The South Korean government is not pleased with the situation either, but is in no position to interfere with the decisions of the judiciary. In 2012, the South Korean Supreme Court declared individual compensation claims admissible before court (*Asahi Shimbun* 10 August 2013).
33. Rome Statute, Art. 79.
34. Coalition for the International Criminal Court, Delivering the Promise of a Fair, Effective and Independent Court: Trust Fund for Victims, http://www.iccnow.org/?mod=trustfund (accessed 6 June 2014).
35. Two thirds of this sum is earmarked for victims of sexual- and gender-based violence. Ministry of Foreign Affairs Japan (7 May 2014), Japan's Contribution to the Trust Fund for Victims (TFV) at the International Criminal Court (ICC), http://www.mofa.go.jp/press/release/press22e_000022.html (accessed 5 June 2014).

References

Amnesty International, 2006 (5 December). *Nihon: kokkai giin ni taishite nihon seifu no kokusai keiji saibanjo setchi kitei (rōma kitei) e no kanyū wo shiji suru yō yobikakeru* (Japan: We call on Diet members to support the Government of Japan's joining the Statute to establish the International Criminal Court [Rome Statute]). Available from: http://www.amnesty.or.jp/news/2006/1205_601.html (Accessed 30 June 2014).

Arai, K., Akira, M., and Osamu, Y., 2008. Japan's accession to the ICC statute and the ICC cooperation law. *Japanese Yearbook of International Law*, 51, 359–383.

Asahi Shimbun, 2013. Rulings on Wartime Compensation Further Sour Tokyo-Seoul Ties (10 August). Available from: http://ajw.asahi.com/article/behind_news/politics/AJ201308100054 (Accessed 5 June 2014).

Bell, D., 2006. *Memory, trauma and world politics: reflections on the relationship between past and present*. Palgrave Macmillan, 1–29.

Berger, T.U., 2009. *Different beds, same nightmare: the politics of history in Germany and Japan* (AICGS Policy Report 39). Baltimore: John Hopkins University.

Berger, T.U., 2012. *War, guilt, and world politics after World War II*. Cambridge: Cambridge University Press.

Bix, H.P., 2000. *Hirohito and the making of modern Japan*. New York: Harper Collins Publishers.

Buruma, I., 2009. *The wages of guilt: memories of war in Germany and Japan* [1994]. London: Atlantic Books.

Cohen, D., 2003. Öffentliche Erinnerung und Kriegsverbrecherprozesse in Asien und Europa. *In*: C. Cornelißen, L. Klinkhammer and W. Schwentker, eds. *Erinnerungskulturen. Deutschland, Italien und Japan seit 1945*. Frankfurt/Main: Fischer, 51–66.

Futamura, M., 2008. *War crimes tribunals and transitional justice. The Tokyo trial and the Nuremberg legacy*. London: Routledge.

Gaimushō, 2012. *Kokusai keiji saibanjo (ICC) to nihon gaikō* (The International Criminal Court (ICC) and Japan's Foreign Policy). Available from: http://www.mofa.go.jp/mofaj/gaiko/icc/pdfs/icc.pdf (Accessed 15 August 2014).

Goold, B., 2002. Ratifying the Rome Statute: Japan and the International Criminal Court. *Asia Pacific Human Rights Information Center Focus*, 29. Available from: http://www.hurights.or.jp/archives/focus/section2/2002/09/ratifying-the-rome-statute-japan-and-the-international-criminal-court.html (Accessed 2 July 2006).

Hein, P., 2010. Patterns of war reconciliation in Japan and Germany: a comparison. *East Asia*, 27 (2), 145–164.

Higashizawa, Y., 2007. *Kokusai keiji saibanjo. Hō to jitsumu* (The International Criminal Court. Law and Practice). Tokyo: Akashi Shoten.

Hyun-ki, K. and Kim, S., 2013. Abe questions Japan's WWII aggression again. *Korea JoongAng Daily* (9 May). Available from: http://koreajoongangdaily.joins.com/news/article/Article.aspx?aid=2971304 (Accessed 31 August 2014).

Inazumi, M., 2008. Japan and the ICC: a reflection from the perspective of the principle of complementarity. *In:* I. Boerefijn and J. Goldschmidt, eds. *Changing Perceptions of Sovereignty and Human Rights: Essays in Honour of Cees Flinterman*. Antwerp: Intersentia, 417–435.

Iwasawa, Y., 1998. *International law, human rights, and Japanese law*. Oxford: Clarendon Press.

Jeffery, R. and H.J. Kim, 2014. New horizons: transitional justice in the Asia-Pacific. *In:* R. Jeffery and H.J. Kim, eds. *Transitional justice in the Asia-Pacific*. Cambridge: Cambridge University Press, 1–31.

Japan Federation of Bar Association, 2002. *Kokusai keiji saibanjo e no nihon no sekkyokuteki sanka wo motomeru ketsugi* (Resolution calling for Japan's active involvement in the ICC). Available from: http://www.nichibenren.or.jp/activity/document/opinion/year/2002/2002_16.html (Accessed 30 May 2014).

Japanese Network for the ICC, 2007. *Japanese accession update – fall 2007* (on file with author).

Kō, K., 2007. Kokusai keiji saibanjo kitei no hijun to tetsuzukihō no kadai (Ratifying the Statute of the International Criminal Court and questions of procedural law). *Hōritsu Jihō*, 79 (4), 37–42.

Kristof, N.D., 1995. Tokyo journal: why a nation of apologizers makes one large exception. *The New York Times*. Available from: http://www.nytimes.com/1995/06/12/world/tokyo-journal-why-a-nation-of-apologizers-makes-one-large-exception.html (Accessed 4 April 2014).

Langebacher, E., 2010. Collective memory as a factor in political culture and international relations. *In:* E. Langenbacher and Y. Shain, eds. *Power and the past: collective memory and international relations*. Washington D.C.: Georgetown University Press, 13–49.

Lebow, R.N., 2006. The memory of politics in postwar Europe. *In:* R.N. Lebow, W. Kansteiner and C. Fogu, eds. *The politics of memory in postwar Europe*. Durham: Duke University Press, 1–39.

Lind, J., (2008). *Sorry states: apologies in international relations*. Ithaca: Cornell University Press.

Lukner, K., 2007. Zwei Stolpersteine und eine Hürde auf dem Weg nach Den Haag: Japan wird Mitglied des Internationalen Strafgerichtshofs. *Asien*, 105, 91–102.

Lukner, K., 2012. Global goals versus bilateral barriers? The International Criminal Court in the context of US relations with Germany and Japan. *Japanese Journal of Political Science*, 13 (1), 83–104.

Martin, A. and Jun K., 2013. Koreans press Japan firms over war claims: victims of forced labor win South Korean court rulings. *The Wall Street Journal*, 19 September. Available from: http://www.theguardian.com/world/2013/jul/11/south-korea-court-japan (Accessed 20 May 2014).

Masaki, Y., 2007. Kokusai keiji saibanjo no nihon no kamei to kokunaihō seibi (Japan's membership in the International Criminal Court and the adjustment of domestic law). *Kokusai Mondai*, 560, 26–34.

Masaki, Y., 2008. Japan's entry to the International Criminal Court and the legal challenges it faced. *Japan Yearbook of International Law*, 51, 409–426.

McCurry, J., 2013. South Korean court orders Japan steel firm to compensate wartime workers. *The Guardian*, 11 July. Available from: http://www.theguardian.com/world/2013/jul/11/south-korea-court-japan (Accessed 31 August 2014).

Meierhenrich, J. and Ko, K., 2009. How do states join the International Criminal Court? The implementation of the Rome statute in Japan. *Journal of International Criminal Justice*, 7 (2), 1–24.

Ministry of Foreign Affairs of Japan, 2002. *Visit of EU Experts on the International Criminal Court (Overview and Assessment)*. Available from: http://www.mofa.go.jp/policy/i_crime/icc/visit0212.html (Accessed 13 August 2014).

Ministry of Foreign Affairs of Japan, 2004. *Visit of EU and ICC Officials to Japan (Overall Assessment)*. Available from: http://www.mofa.go.jp/policy/i_crime/icc/visit0412.html (Accessed 13 August 2014).

Moriyama, M., 2007. PGA no sōkai wo owatte (Ending the PGA's General Assembly Meeting). *Ayumi*, 102, 6.

Nakauchi, Y., 2007. Kokusai shakai ni okeru hō no shihai no kakuritsu ni mukete – kokusai keiji saibanjo rōma kitei, kokusai keiji saibanjo kyōryoku hōan no kokkai rongi (Establishing the Rule of Law in the International Community Parliamentary Debate on ICC Cooperation Bill), *Hōritsu to Chōsa*, 270 (7), 3–11.

Nihon Keizai Shinbun, 2007. Nihon no yakuwari to sekinin ga omoi (Japan's role and responsibility are great). *Nihon Keizai Shinbun*, 1 July, p. 2.

Niikura, O., 2007. Kokusai keiji saibanjo kitei no hijun to kokunai hō seibi no kadai (The ratification of the rules of the International Criminal Court and the challenge to establish national law). *Hōritsu Jihō*, 79 (4), 25–30.

Noguchi, M., 2006. Kokusai keiji saibanjo wa ima – nihon no kamei ga hatasu imi (The International Criminal Court is Now: The Significance of Japan's Membership). *Ronza*, 1, 240–247.

Okazaki, Y., 2007. Kokusai keiji saibanjo (ICC) kitei he no kamei to kongo ni mukete. ICC no kongo no kadai to waga kuni no yakuwari (Turning towards the Membership in International Criminal Court and the Future. The ICC's Future Problems and the Role of our Country). *Hōritsu no Hiroba*, 60 (9), 48–53.

Onishi, N., 2007. Decades after war trials, Japan still honors a dissenting judge. *The New York Times*, 31 August. Available from: http://www.nytimes.com/2007/08/31/world/asia/31memo.html?_r=0 (Accessed 31 August 2007).

Osten, P., 2003. *Der Tokioter Kriegsverbrecherprozess und die japanische Rechtswissenschaft*. Berlin: Berliner Wissenschaftsverlag.

Owada, H. and Shibahara K., 1999. Rōma kaigi wo furikakete (Looking back at the Rome Conference). *Jurisuto*, 1146, 4–28.

Pace, W., 2006. Serious progress achieved at April ICC "PrepCom". *The International Criminal Court Monitor*, 1.

Saiki, N., 2002. Zadankai: Nipponhō no kokusaika (Round Table: Internationalization of Japanese Law). *Juristo*, 1232, 6–35.

Sakaki, A., 2012. Japanese-South Korean textbook talks: the necessity of political leadership. *Pacific Affairs*, 85 (2), 263–285.

Schabas, W.A., 2004. *An introduction to the International Criminal Court*. Cambridge University Press.

Simma, B., 1999. The impact of Nuremberg and Tokyo: attempts at a comparison. *In:* Nisuke Ando, ed. *Japan and international law. Past, present and future*. The Hague: Kluwer Law International, 50–84.

Suzuki, M., 2008. Kokusai keiji saibanjo kitei to kokunai ho: Doitsu to nihon wo rei ni [The Statute of the International Criminal Court and domestic law: Germany and Japan as examples]. *In:* Nihon Bengoshi Rengōkai, ed. *Kokusai Keiji Saibanjo no tobira wo akeru* (Open the Door of the International Criminal Court). Tokyo: Gendaijin Bunsha, 120–135.

Tanaka, Y., 2006. Crime and responsibility: war, the state, and Japanese society. *Japan Focus*. Available from: http://www.japanfocus.org/-Yuki-TANAKA/2200 (Accessed 2 May 2014).

Togo, K., 2008. Japan's historical memory: overcoming polarization toward synthesis. *In:* T. Hasegawa and K. Togo, eds. *East Asia's haunted present: historical memories and the resurgence of nationalism.* Westport: Praeger Security International, 597–599.

Togo, K., 2010. Japan's historical memory toward the United States. *In:* Gilbert Rozman, ed. *U.S. leadership, history, and bilateral relations in Northeast Asia.* Cambridge: Cambridge University Press, 17–44.

Totani, Y., 2009. *The Tokyo War crimes trial. The pursuit of justice in the wake of World War II.* Cambridge (MA): Harvard University Press.

Wellenstein, E., 2004. *EU-Japan ICC Dialogue: Introductory Statement/Press Briefing by Edmond H. Wellenstein, Director General Ministry of Foreign Affairs of the Netherlands (Tokyo, 1 December).* Available from: http://www.consilium.europa.eu/uedocs/cmsupload/icceu%20press%20briefing.pdf (Accessed 13 August 2014).

Yamada, S., 2014. True face of Chinese plaintiffs seeking wartime compensation for Forced Labor. *Nikkei Asian Review* (16 May). Available from: http://asia.nikkei.com/Politics-Economy/Policy-Politics/True-face-of-Chinese-plaintiffs-seeking-wartime-compensation-for-forced-labor (Accessed 5 June 2014).

Contested memories of the Kamikaze and the self-representations of Tokkō-tai youth in their missives home

LULI VAN DER DOES-ISHIKAWA

The word Kamikaze has haunted the image of Japan abroad and at home, producing tales, legends, and internet memes, embedding itself in today's youth culture. The contested memories of the Kamikaze ascribe them various identities and their associated characterization continues to evolve, but mostly in the absence of their own self-identity. This cross-disciplinary study explores the Kamikaze's self-representation in their own words and aims to trace the sources of the contested memories in the sociopolitical conditioning that was present at the time the discourse was produced. In the course of this empirical study a central theme emerges: the struggle for self-identity anchored in 'home and family' associated with frequent reference to 'being and thinking'. A diversity of beliefs and backgrounds of the Tokkō-tai youth is uncovered. The findings of the quantitative data analysis are then subjected to detailed critical discourse analysis to explore, through multifaceted contextualization, the socio-cognitive link among Kamikazes' self-images, education and training in contrast to their younger peers. Shifts in the social context, agency and norms have shaped, through conceptual association and assimilation, peers' interpretation of the Kamikaze's (self-) representation over time, eventually giving rise to the sources of ongoing memory debate concerning the identity and images associated with the Kamikaze.

'The past is a foreign country: they do things differently there'
(Hartley 1953, p. 1)

Introduction

Leo, in *The Go-between* (Hartley 1953) and a woman in *A Pale View of Hills* (Ishiguro 1982) both wrestle with recollections. As they talk from their memories, by shifting emphasis and reference points, they create a distance between themselves and past events. Eventually, different versions of the past emerge. Leo, towards the end of his life, confronts the past, while the woman remains in a world of dissociation, even from her own name.

When recalled events stir emotional discomfort, the human psyche protects itself with detachment and dissociation (Douglas and Marmar 2002). Yet denial of the facts of our past, our roots, threatens our self-preservation, and puts our self-identity at risk. So we negotiate between 'continuity' to counter 'unsettling change' by insisting on the 'bond between our present selves and a certain fragment of the past' on one hand and 'discontinuity' to emphasize our 'separation from what we have lost' whether factual or imagined on the other (Atia and Davies 2010, p. 184). Nostalgia also shapes historical memory (Hodgins 2004) by editing facts to fit into a preferred framework. We may forget certain aspects of a past event, recall it from different viewpoints, or deny any involvement altogether. The psychological distance of time, space, and social standing from the past manifests itself linguistically (Brown 1995) and indexical linguistic behaviour illuminates how we view an event (Filmore 1971) from first, second, or third-person perspectives. Thus, one factual event may instantiate an infinite number of memories depending on our viewpoint and, more importantly, on the information available at the time we evaluate the past. No wonder the thousands of youths, called Tokkō-tai, or known as *Kamikaze* in English, who were sent on suicide missions have continued to produce contested memories ascribing to them numerous versions of their presumed identities and intentions for their infamous deeds.

This study explores the characterization of the Kamikaze given to them in their contested memories and compares it with the self-representation in the texts of authentic missives written by the Kamikaze themselves, considering 'who they are' when described from second- and third-person perspectives in contrast to 'who I am' as traced in the missives in the first-person. Similarities and differences are identified and contextualized, and an explanation is sought for in their sociocognitive conditioning, such as their education and training. Global implications are drawn from the empirical results for the importance of evidence-based study for the attainment of a fuller memory of the Tokkō-tai youth. Section 2 reviews the major streams of Kamikaze characterization in contested, collective and individual Kamikaze memories. Section 3 reports on the empirical study of the missives home written by the Kamikaze pilots. Layers of Kamikaze discourse are identified: the authors' self-representation contained in Kamikaze missives (the texts) is teased out from their social representations (how they are interpreted and characterized by different audiences in a given time and space) and the discursive social practice (how they are presented and communicated). The letters are analysed using an interdisciplinary methodology yielding thematic characterization of the missives' contents. The missives' dominant themes turned out to be self-identity linked to *furusato* (one's 'home' or 'hometown') on one hand and the paucity of belligerent expressions against, and clear identification of, the 'enemy' on the other. Section 4 discusses the cognitive link between the missives and the education system of the period as an integral part of Imperial Japan's Family-Nation ideology and the strategy of *shisō-sen* ('Thought War') (Nishio 1943, Kushner 2006), that shaped the perspectives of the Kamikaze's younger peers, leading them to establish one of the most dominant discourses in the post-war memories of the Kamikaze. The final section discusses the future risk of abuse of the Kamikaze concept in the absence of a factual reference point, as seen in internet memes and social media, and which proliferates through the assimilation and association of related discourse. This empirical, comprehensive and contextualized re-evaluation of the missives provides a primary source for interpreting the self-identity of the Tokkō-tai in the context of the collective memory.

Who they are: contested memories of Tokkō-tai youth

In English, *Kamikaze* is a generic term associated with a variety of suicidal actions and is frequently found in internet discourse today. A simple keyword search returns millions of hits with associated sub-themes varying from light-hearted jokes about self-inflicted disaster, the motto of a youth football club, the title of a rom-com manga, recruitment adverts for diverse organizations of varied causes to the Syrian army (Mahmood and Booth 2013), and most recently, the 'Kami-Crazy' kids in Mad Max: Fury Road (Truitt 2015).

Evolving 'Kamikaze' memes and associated images in the media

The term 'Kamikaze' is no longer confined to its original, Japanese, proper noun form, with a specific etymology, but has evolved into a meme, which is constantly augmented by its users. An example is found in online news: 'The Japanese referee died as a Kamikaze for Brazil' (FOCUS Online 2014). During the 2014 World Cup's, Brazil vs. Croatia match, a Japanese referee gave a penalty to Brazil, sparking criticism in both conventional and social media. Here, the associated images are of self-sacrifice to appease a party (Brazil, the host nation) out of obligation. Another usage of 'kamikaze' might be to suggest a suicidal (or unreasonable) offensive strategy in management as in a news article, 'Sir Alex Ferguson has accused some of Manchester United's rivals of going on a "kamikaze" spending spree' (Press Association 2010), where the term is used as an adjective. 'Kamikaze' can also be understood as a verb in English, as in a poster produced by an online shop shown in Figure 1 (Keep Calm Network Ltd n.d.).[1]

Memes also spread with visual associations, as in Kamikaze pictures parodying the popular TV series *Game of Thrones* (http://frabz.com/2qxy) or the joke/discussion 'Why Did Kamikaze pilots wear helmets?' (Adams 1994, jimikelso 2012, Soniak 2013), which has been around for decades and keeps resurfacing online with new images (http://www.memecenter.com/fun/241649/kamikaze) and associated meanings. These memes invite 'likes' and comments and are shared

Figure 1 Keep Calm meme
Source: Keep Calm Network Ltd

instantaneously. Social media has produced numerous Kamikaze-themed clips, with 27,000,000 videos on YouTube alone (June 2014). In fact, the majority are Kamikaze-inspired creations without substantial relevance to the original Second World War soldiers, but they keep evolving, acquiring new meanings and associated memories, specific to the given context, population, and time. While memes are user-led and appear spontaneously online in an unpredictable manner, the image of the Kamikaze can also be disseminated in controlled media expression. Examples are the two Japanese blockbuster films in 2013 that sparked renewed popularity of the Kamikaze: 'Kaze-tachinu (known as Wind Arises)' by Miyazaki Hayao and 'The Eternal 0 (Eien no zero)' based on Hyakuta Naoki's multi-million bestseller, both associated with 'the notion that Japan is still significant even though its international competitiveness has been weakening' (Yanagida 2014). Fansubs (the subtitling of foreign, especially animated, films by fans) in various languages are uploaded continuously, showing the unstoppability of Kamikaze-related information in both legal and illegal channels worldwide. A Korean newspaper, Hankyoreh, reports the heightened popularity of Kamikaze-related entertainment books, games, and plastic models of battleships and fighter aircraft, criticizing Japan's recent 'intoxication' with the dogfighter 'Zero' as dangerous 'blind nostalgia for the past' despite the aircraft's design of prioritizing efficiency at the cost of safety (Kil 2014).

The popularity of the Kamikaze theme, however, does not equate with a national endorsement of suicide missions. Traditional mass media, such as NHK (Nihon Hōsō Kyōkai: the national broadcasting company), ran a series of Kamikaze-inspired programmes, some of which offered alternative views of historical facts. On social media vibrant debates rolled out (https://twitter.com/hashtag/特攻隊?mode = news), many of which discussed the revived interest in the Kamikaze and its impact on international relations triggered by social media. Concerns are expressed for the gap between today's inflated interpretations of the Kamikaze memories and the historical facts being a possible source for international conflict.

The original meaning of 'Kamikaze' in Japanese

Confusion surrounds the meaning of the term 'Kamikaze', which in English is a hypernym for suicide attacks carried out by: explosive-laden aircraft, torpedoes, submarines, speed boats, and divers. These are, in fact, an incorrect adaptation of the Japanese proper noun, which has a narrow reference. The general term should be '*Tokkō-tai* (Special Attack Unit)'. '*Kamikaze/Shinpū* 神風', literally meaning 'god/spirit wind', usually translated into English as 'divine wind', is reserved for a specific squadron of the Imperial Japanese Navy Air Force. The Army Air Force *Tokkō-tai* had its own name, '*Shinbu-tai*' (lit. Military force). This gross English simplification is in part the source of the misattribution of the 'Kamikaze' memories to the wrong referent.

The etymology of Kamikaze in Japanese can be found in a thirteenth century legend, whereby god-sent typhoons saved Japan from two Mongol invasions, sinking the enemy fleet. The typhoons became known as '*Shinpū* (lit. god-wind)', after which the Navy *Tokkō-tai* were named. As the word 'wind' in Japanese is associated with 'destiny', the pilots were said to fulfil divine will, which is the origin of the Kamikaze's legendary/religious connotation.

Controversy of 'forget-me-not'

One of the pilots, M.S., 20 years old, wrote: 'Brother, whenever the radio sounds, remember me'. In our memories of the Kamikaze can a message of 'forget-me-not' occupy any space at all? So far, their memories are, by definition, founded on second and third-person perspectives. For the last 70 years they have been characterized variously as, extremists, fanatics, martyrs, heroes dedicated to self-sacrificing acts of honour, young victims of brain-washing by a totalitarian government, or a blueprint of workaholics in today's corporate Japan, to name but a few. The very word evokes Japan's unresolved war responsibilities as both perpetrator and victim amongst the countless numbers of casualties. Memories of the kamikaze are rarely studied by themselves, as they are, but are almost always intertwined with war memories of Japan in the context of East Asia. Therefore, we will briefly review the characterization of the Kamikaze along the lines of Dower's (2012, p. 112) five kinds of war memory in Japan: (1) denial; (2) evocations of moral (or immoral) equivalence; (3) victim consciousness; (4) binational (US–Japan) sanitizing of Japanese war crimes; and (5) popular discourses acknowledging guilt and responsibility.

Debates concerning memories of the Kamikaze resurged in 2014 amid the controversies surrounding the territorial dispute over the Senkaku-Daioyu islands and the Abe government's visits to the Yasukuni shrine: the Minami-Kagoshima municipality submitted a collection of 'Kamikaze [sic] soldiers' personal effects and last letters home, stored in the municipality's Chiran Peace Memorial Museum, for entry into UNESCO's Memory of the World programme. China and South Korea also applied, with material on the comfort women, refuelling heated scholarly and media-based debates on the Japanese government's handling of war memories in East Asia and whether submitting these letters to this programme amounted to a justification of Imperial Japan's war conduct. The application was rejected on 17 June by the Japanese National Commission for UNESCO on the grounds that the Chiran Collection did not meet the criteria set by UNESCO in terms of representing sufficiently diverse viewpoints.

Those supporting Chiran maintain that respecting and remembering the war-dead does not constitute justification of the atrocities of war (Homepage, Chiran Peace Memorial Museum 2014), but critics equate this logic with the negation of Japan's war responsibilities in the Pacific War, which are associated not only with the suicide attacks but also with the unresolved issues of the forced labour of Koreans, Comfort Women, or the Nanjing Massacre. Here, the Kamikaze memories are state-oriented: memories of individuals may be ignored and subsumed into the collective international memory of the condemnation of Japan's war responsibility. Denial of Japan's war responsibility is ascribed to the presumed identity of the Kamikaze and the contents of their missives.

Immediately after Chiran's application, criticisms flooded the internet. In an article entitled 'Flying in the face of reason' (Zongduo 2014) the application was condemned as 'Japan's attempt to glorify its kamikaze pilots of World War II [and] is a brazen violation of universal human values', whereby 'One tragedy of World War II was Japan's fascist fanatics driving young pilots into suicidal attacks on US warships'. The collective memory of the Kamikaze, according to the author, is that 'these kamikaze attacks have become synonymous with *crazy, reckless behavior* (Zongduo 2014, Author's emphasis)'. Notably, the said article concentrates on the controversial, nationalist movements, without mentioning the actual diversity in Japanese domestic views on Tokkō-tai:

> ...For today's Japanese nationalists, the kamikaze pilots... embody Japan's samurai warrior spirit of devotion and revenge and therefore should be idolized... The fact that their action [the UNESCO application] received little objection in Japan highlights a disturbing trend: The fetish for war extremism has spread from Tokyo officials to local intellectuals after campaigns fanned by right-wing winds, and the kamikaze attacks are no longer viewed as acts of madness by the Japanese military. (Zongduo 2014)

As witnessed above, the individual memories of the Tokkō-tai appear to be overridden by the debate about Japan's war responsibility in the international memory of the Kamikazes. Their presumed identities are 'crazy, reckless' and 'embody Japan's samurai warrior spirit of devotion and revenge and therefore should be idolized'. Moral and immoral equivalence are evoked. A shallowness and belligerence of character is presumed, with a suggestion of a lack of capacity to make decisions. In the context of the UNESCO application the said characteristics of the Kamikaze are also assumed to mirror their missives without any evidence to substantiate the claim. Lack of direct access to the majority of their missives may also be the cause.

There is also a deep-seated suspicion about the authenticity of the letters in the Chiran collection. Critics state that 'the letters and documents are real in handwriting but hardly in thinking... Due to the Imperial Army codes of behavior and peer pressure, those young pilots…could *never* express their agony, doubts and concerns in words as it would threaten the lives of their immediate families and other relatives' (Zongduo 2014, Author's emphasis). This characterization is based on an assumed 'victim consciousness' whereby the identity of the Kamikaze is that of conformists, emotionally suppressed and controlled, and the same characteristic is assumed to be present in their writing, again without any evidence. Censorship and psychological pressure on the young recruits volunteering to become Tokkō are well documented and the writing of 'will's "under duress"' (Ohnuki-Tierney 2004) may well have occurred. However, not all missives are official and censored. So far, except for the thorough anthropological studies of six authentic Kamikaze-diaries (Ohnuki-Tierney 2004) the majority of claims about the contents of the Kamikaze letters are speculative, often based on public opinion and the small volume of exhibits at war memorial museums, which were purposefully selected for public view in line with the museum's exhibition themes. Meanwhile, the 'orthodoxy' among the English-speaking media portrays Japanese war memory as either a 'state-centred' approach focusing on the official narrative of the Japanese government or a 'culturally-determinist' approach that blames 'the conformist nature of Japan's group society' for assumed consensus on individual views (Seaton 2007a, pp. 2–3) and so the international image of the Kamikaze has been disseminated and established.

While the characterization of the Kamikaze within the international collective memory, based on the notion of Japan as the aggressor, is relatively unified, in contrast, the positioning of the Kamikaze in Japanese domestic war memory is highly contested, reflecting, on a public level, divergent Japanese public opinions on the morality of Japan's war conduct and intention, and, curiously, an additional sociolinguistic element of 'empathy' on the personal level. Also, while a consensus can be broadly reached concerning Japan's aggressive actions during the war, Japanese opinion is split in two regarding the intentions of the war. The progressives renounce Japan's conduct as a war of aggression with a clear intention to invade; a crime against international peace in the sense of the United Nations Resolution 3314 (Ogawa 2014, p. 52) by which the Kamikaze Tokkō-tai is regarded as a symbolic example of the state's crimes committed against its own people. This is a popular discourse of an acknowledgment of guilt and responsibility coupled with victim consciousness (Dower 2012, p. 112). In contrast, the nationalists take the stance of denial (Dower 2012, p. 112) considering the same war as, at most, an act of aggression with internationally historical and political reasons that necessitated Japan's actions, with the Kamikaze being an inevitable consequence and a honourable display of national spirit (Abe 2006, p. 107). Views of war responsibility in education – such as the *shisōsen* that mobilized the youth through education and propaganda are also at stake. The teachers' unions have led public opinion in this regard since the 1950s, but the unity against nationalism in the classroom has eroded since the 1990s. Reminiscent of the popularity of 'victorious' World War Mangas during the 1950–60s (Nakar 2003), stories with heroic images of the Tokkō-tai are gaining popularity, suggesting the emergence of a new collective domestic memory of the Kamikaze. Adding to the debate is the problematic application of legal concepts. Nationalists refer to the fact that the 1946 International Military Tribunal for the Far East, and not the non-binding 1974 UN resolution, found Japan to have committed a 'war of aggression' applying *ex-post facto* law (Lukner, in this issue), calling it 'victors' justice' to support the discourse of denial. Others relate this to the discourse of victimization by the 'victors', but usually the Kamikaze does not figure in these arguments. Scholars who point to the binational sanitizing of Japanese war crimes at the Tribunal (Dower 2012), however, question whether the inclusion of class-A war criminals in the Yasukuni shrine next to the Tokkō war-dead is part of the process of this sanitization (Sakaguchi 2005, pp. 15–16).

Yasukuni jinja

The aforementioned Chiran's move has been compared, in the international media, to the revisionist historiography observed in Yūshūkan, the Yasukuni's war memorial museum; its 'Kamikaze' letter exhibits have been criticized as nationalist propaganda for the glorification of war within the museum's distorted historical representation (O'Dwyer 2010) and as a symbol of revisionism set against the responsible and progressive manifestation of Japan's war memory. Yūshūkan's perceived 'denial' (Dower 2012) is translated into the assumption that the texts of the Tokkō-tai missives themselves are also imbued with imperialism, militarism and nationalist propaganda. At the same time, the same exhibits are observed as exerting a humanistic appeal to Japan's contemporary culture, whereby the tragedy of ordinary youth, as depicted in the letters, would invoke an intense and visceral emotional response in the audience, arousing a feeling of 'gratitude' towards the heroes (Sakamoto 2014). As such, views on Kamikaze memories diverge, but the awareness of their international impact is shared across the population. There are a 'multiplicity' of views of Yasukuni (Havlíček 2009, p. 70) and the 'dilemma of talismanic symbolism' (Kingston 2007) that continues to divide public opinion about its role in war memory and in society at large. Given the diversity of public opinion, the Japanese government has taken a cautious approach to clarifying its views on the war memories and politicians' Yasukuni shrine visits. Constitutional divisions between state and religion as well as the impact on international relations are at issue. While some consider that international intervention constitutes a violation of freedom of religion (Okuyama 2009), others call for a 'voluntary restraint' in the light of regional international relations. A survey in January 2014 showed that 46 per cent of Japanese respondents considered PM Abe should not have visited the Yasukuni Shrine, while 41 per cent supported it. Further, 51 per cent said Japan should take the criticisms from China, Korea, USA, and Russia seriously, while 40 per cent disagreed, and 9 per cent were undecided. Among those against the PM's Yasukuni visit, 80 per cent expressed concerns about the international criticism (Asahi-Shimbun 2014). The public is more unified over the honouring (not glorifying) of the war-dead. 50 per cent supported the idea of creating a new, non-religious memorial, away from the Yasukuni Shrine, while only 29 per cent disagreed, and 21 per cent was undecided. The public wishes to pay respect to the war-dead separately from the 'state-religion' Shintō, or international politics, including the issues of war responsibility. This may indicate the Japanese preference for separating issues of collective and individual memories. Perhaps the most prevalent domestic feeling for the Kamikaze is that of sympathy for the fallen, regardless of their war conduct, as if death provides immunity from judgement by the living, a sentiment often expressed at memorial museums.

Museums

Memorial museums have the potential to provide visitors with opportunities to consider the factual representations of war memories (Yoshida 2007, 2013). In this regard the museums' representation of war memories are split into two types: 'war' museums that do not acknowledge Japan's wartime aggression, and 'peace' museums that ostensibly do the opposite (Jeans 2005). Since the two major museums that exhibit Kamikaze missives are categorized as being the former type, the texts of Kamikaze missives tend to be automatically ascribed the role of advancing the position of the 'denial' or 'victimization' discourse. However, some studies touch upon the texts of the missives themselves, noting their 'affective economy' of strong humanistic appeal (Sakamoto 2014). With the help of linguistic familiarity, the Japanese-speaking public can appreciate the contents of the Kamikaze missives home far more readily than the international audience. They can take stock of subtle nuances and contextual information, which are abundant within their own society, for deeper discourse comprehension. Thus, such an audience can focus on the Kamikazes' individual memories apart from the exhibition setting and without recontextualizing it within other background knowledge. The physical context in which a letter is placed often clouds the readers' view, giving an overriding impression of the letter without careful attention to what its text actually says in a larger context. Exhibits at the Chiran and Yasukuni's museums are displayed in a theme-based design concept. If the theme was the soldiers' self-sacrifice for the country, only the relevant extracts from a collection of letters are carefully selected, arranged, and exhibited representing the 'preferred discourse' (Fairclough 1989) to advance the agenda of the design concept, forming a gestalt of collective memory. The notable absence of the ordinary features of a personal letter or mundane reports of daily life as well as both the positive and negative emotions among the exhibits of Yūshūkan (Sakamoto 2014) may or may not be intentional but, in any case, the very act of thematic presentation itself controls the scope of represented viewpoints, and consequently offers a one-sided view. Therefore, the way the Kamikaze missives are presented in thematic museums should not be confused with what the missives actually say in their entirety.

Indeed, empathy, which requires highly complex sociolinguistic and cognitive communicative knowledge of a particular language culture, plays a greater role in interpreting the missives. Jeans' (2005, p. 155) attention to the details of contextualization is insightful. He describes his emotional response to a letter from a Kamikaze pilot who had a partial French lineage, saying: 'it was painful to think how intense the pressure must have been to prove himself 100 percent Japanese by volunteering' as a Special Attack pilot. This sharply contrasts with Buruma's account of Japanese pilots' missives exhibited at Chiran: 'for the phony ideals and the saccharine poetics are ... part of the place ... the blurbs about "beauty in the laughing faces" the stuff in the museum guide about this being a "hall of tears"; the ghastly oil painting ... of a dead pilot being lifted to heaven from his burning plane by ... [definitely Asian] angels...' (Buruma 1994, p. 227). His choice of the word, 'saccharin', indicates the assumption that the Kamikaze poetic writings may well be artificial, but what if, instead, they were authentic and genuinely written by the young boys, even though too clumsily for his literary taste? This urges us to investigate the original texts of the missives. Can cultural context profoundly influence the impression of the text? Compare the following.

A Kamikaze wrote: 'I am going to make a sortie... This is the last, mother... the Captain said "as we go out to fight, the life and death of our family nation (*kokka*) is on our shoulders"... So, Mum please rejoice for me. Your son has become a proper man now... as I can never forget you, I will be always in your heart... Laugh. I was a funny guy, wasn't I? Mother, I will dive into the enemy ship, embracing your gentle smile in my heart'[2] (NY 1945).

The poetic offering of another soldier goes: 'And we held on to each other / Like brother to brother / We promised our mothers we'd write / And we would all go down together... Yes, we would all go down together / Remember... / They left their childhood / ... And who was wrong? / And who was right? / It didn't matter in the thick of the fight.'

The essence of the above is found in the following verse: 'If this is to end in fire / Then we should all burn together /... And if we should die tonight / Then we should all die together / Raise a glass of wine for the last time / Calling out father, prepare as we will.'

Of the above three, the second is from Billy Joel's great US hit from 1983, "Good night Saigon"[3], contextualized within the Vietnam War (http://www.billyjoel.com/music/kohuept/goodnight-saigon). The third is the greatest international hit of 2013–14 with 121,335,760 viewings as of 1 July 2015 on Youtube alone (https://www.youtube.com/watch?v=ngvQS_PmQ). The song is from "I see fire" by Ed Sheeran (2013)[4] (http://www.edsheeran.com/) and is contextualized in the war that the Hobbits waged in Tolkien's story. To most of us, the Hobbits do not constitute any national or racial group and, therefore, are the easiest of the three above to empathize with globally. This reminds us that both in the context of the museum exhibition and in the historical context in which it was written, the teasing apart of the layers of contextualization will be the key to finding the (self-)identities of the Kamikaze.

Letters

In search of genuine individual memories of the Kamikazes, Tanaka (2005) studied records and letters of the young non-commissioned petty officers, who formed more than two-thirds of the total Kamikaze pilots. He found no strong evidence of belligerent language or hatred in the texts, but observed five dominant characteristic features: (1) rationalizing one's own death to defend one's country and its people; (2) the belief that to die for the 'country' was to show filial piety to one's own parents, particularly to one's mother; (3) strong solidarity with their flight-mates who shared their fate as Kamikaze pilots; (4) a strong sense of responsibility and contempt for cowardice; and, (5) a lack of an image of the enemy (Tanaka 2005). These findings appear to suggest the concept of 'self' in the missives is closely linked to the society in which the Kamikaze lived. This link may be a key to understanding how Kamikazes represented themselves and how that became the source of today's contested memories. Issues 'closest to home – family, friends and *furusato* (home town/area) – affect Japanese war memories' and 'family and local identities impinge on the evolution of cultural memory and war commemoration' (Seaton 2007b). Here, the concept of '*furusato*' is especially loaded with emotional and nostalgic associations that have been used politically to unite the nation (Robertson 1988). If so, the manipulation of the '*furusato*' concept in association with the Kamikaze memories can create divergent nationalistic memories. On the other hand, the concept of nostalgia for home can have universal appeal. Even though there is a wide range of individual experiences, fundamental notions such as 'home' and 'self' permeate across individual memories regardless of national backgrounds.

Indeed, Tokkō-tai consisted not only of Japanese but also of Korean recruits. Park Dongfun was a Tokkō-tai pilot of the 'Shinbu' Unit of the Imperial Army whose Will, exhibited in the Chiran Peace Memorial Museum, reads 'kesshi決死', literally, sure-death, which can be variously translated as: a lethal attack, resolutely prepared, mortal struggle, suicide squad, and so on. He had accepted the mission on the assurance of his superior in the Imperial Army that his family would be taken care of (Kil 2010). Another Korean officer, Lieutenant Noh Younwu of the Imperial Army, died crashing his own plane on a B29 and became revered as a *Gun-shin*, (lit. military-god, or divine martyr), which is the Japanese military version of his individual memory. His mother died in 1988 believing her son to be alive somewhere in a foreign country, and his remains were returned to his sister in 2005 when she finally learnt the circumstances of his death. A little note from his 'sister' was found in his breast pocket, possibly from his lover of whom they never knew (Kil 2010). Thus, each 'Kamikaze' formed a part of the collective memories and individual memories simultaneously, having layers of both national and individual identity. Therefore, a multi-dimensional rapprochement between collectivist vs. individualist memories (Olick 1999) is called for. By shifting the focus from national identity to individual identity and re-examining Kamikaze identities in contested memories, complex layers of factors and viewpoints that form the memories will become elucidated, allowing an examination of facts against defined parameters. So far, the above discussions have yielded the following four areas of characterization.

1. Actions under duress. Lack of responsibility and authority to make choices — age, rank.
2. Intellectual and psychological weakness. Naïve, brain-washed, conformist — educational background.
3. Extremism. Fanatic Shintoists, emperor-worship — religious affiliation/linguistic contents.
4. Ideological contents of the missives manifested in linguistic contents displaying:

    4(a) belligerence and hatred against enemies.
    4(b) prominent topics of imperialism, militarism, or ultranationalism.
    4(c) self-identity intertwined with 4(a) and 4(b).

These premises will be empirically tested through the study of a large collection of authentic Kamikaze missives in the next section.

Past: who am I?

This section examines the authentic writings of the Kamikazes themselves, using a quantitative and qualitative hybrid analytical framework to test the applicability of the features discussed in the previous section.

Quantitative characterization of the missives' authors

The exact number of the Tokkō-tai war-dead is unknown, but available historical records point to approximately 6000 (Tokko-tai Senbotsusha Irei Heiwa Kinen Kyokai 2008) imperial army and navy combined. Counting every single soldier involved in any suicidal mission raises the figure up to 15,000: this includes everyone from foot soldiers at the frontlines to crews of submarines and warships that transported airplanes or small submarines for Tokkō missions. This article's focus, the official figures of the Imperial Navy Tokkō-tai war-dead, totals 4156

(Tokko-tai Senbotsusha Irei Heiwa Kinen Kyokai 2008), consisting of *Kaiten* (manned torpedoes), *Shinyō* (motorboats with bow-mounted explosives), *Kōhyōteki* (midget submarines) representing 104, 1081, and 440 men respectively, as well as the 2531 pilots, called the *Shinpū*, a.k.a. 'Kamikaze', squadron. The sample size of the missives required to represent Shinpū at a confidence level of 95 per cent and a 5 per cent confidence interval is 322, and 342 to statistically represent the entire Navy Tokkō-tai. This study randomly selected 828 documents from the Ōmi Collection, which resulted in 379 missives consisting of 181 letters, 118 postcards, and eighty poems to satisfy the confidence level and interval. To profile the Kamikazes, their age at their last mission, educational background, and religious affiliation were analysed. Secondly, the contents of the missives were analysed for word frequency and distribution taking into account semantic networks.

Demographic study

The initial results disclosed a diverse demography in the discourse contents, whereas the literacy level and linguistic contents were homogeneous. All tables and graphs, except Figure 10A, are by the author.

1. Age distribution

Descriptive statistics on age are as shown in Table 1 and graphically represented in the histogram below (Figure 2).

The age of Tokkō-tai ranged from 15 to 39 years. The mean (average) age was 20.9 years with a standard deviation of 2.87 years. Those aged 22 years and less represented 75 per cent of the total. The mode (most frequently occurring) age was 19 years. The discrepancies between and among the mean, mode and median values here reflects a distribution skewed towards the lower value (i.e. younger). Regarding Premise 1, the majority of Kamikaze pilots were too young to hold authoritative ranks but, having passed puberty, were considered to be old enough to make personal-level decisions.

Table 1 Age distribution

Mean age	20.9 years
Standard deviation	2.872 years
Age range	15 to 39 years
Median	20 years
Mode	19 years
Percentiles 25 per cent	19
50 per cent	20
75 per cent	22
Skewness	2.562

Source: Author

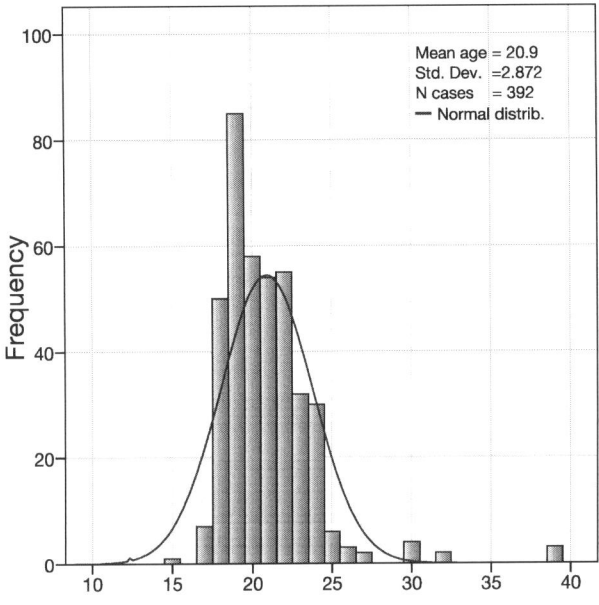

Figure 2 Age distribution
Source: Author

2. The educational background of the Kamikazes

The Kamikazes' backgrounds are diverse (Figure 3): *Yoka-ren* (Navy fast track pilot course) 62 per cent, *Futsū-ka* (student pilot and engineer of the Navy School) 7.1 per cent, *Hei-Gakkō* (Navy Officer School) 5.6 per cent, and *Gakuto* (University and Teacher-Training College Students) 22.7 per cent, with 2.6 per cent undocumented. The *Hei-gakkō* graduates were highly-trained elites, but Japan had lost the majority of its skilled pilots in the battles of Midway and the Solomon Islands by the time the 1943 Student-Mobilization Law was issued. In the final years of the war, most Kamikazes received minimal training before their final mission, due to sheer lack of instructors, resources, and manpower. For example, the students of *Yoka-ren*, the 'fast track pilot course', received only one-year's training, which, later, was further reduced to six months (Takahashi 2013, p. 76). While they received only enough training to be able to fly an airplane, highly skilled pilots were assigned to 'escort' the Kamikazes to the proximity of the target fleet. Consequently, the Kamikazes largely consisted of young and hastily-trained pilots, as well as recently-recruited university graduates. The notion of 'disposable' lives in versions of Kamikaze memory emerged from here.

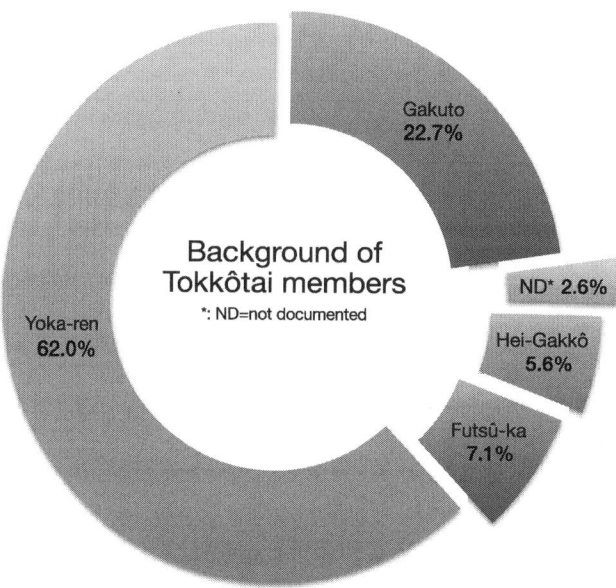

Figure 3 Educational background
Source: Author

The educational background as well as the age distribution may also have affected the content of the missives. Figure 4 shows that *Yoka-ren* pilots are the youngest of the four groups. Again, the discrepancies between the mean and mode values in *Futsū-ka* and *Yoka-ren* explain the skewness towards the lower value, that most Kamikaze individuals were 20 years of age or younger.

The time-frame of the Tokkō-tai missives is from 11 November, 1941, with the official naming of the *Kōhyōteki* midget submarines as the Special Attack Unit, until Japan's surrender on 15 August 1945. The number of missives written during the time-frame of March–June 1945, when the most deadly battles in Okinawa were fought, greatly increased (Figure 5). The memory of the battle still lives in the political, international, and social contexts of the Okinawan identity (Hook, this issue).

A closer look at this particular period (Figure 6) reveals that the authors of missives during the peak were circa 20 years old, of which the majority of individuals (shown by the mode) were even younger.

These results portray a group of young adults with diverse educational backgrounds, refuting Premise 2 that assumes, homogenously, the 'un-educated, naïve, brain-washed' identities of the Kamikaze youth. Their age range will provide a crucial socio-cognitive context when analysing the discourse of their missives qualitatively in Section 4. Controversies about the Kamikaze memories often relate to the Yasukuni-shrine issues, and therefore their religious background is examined next.

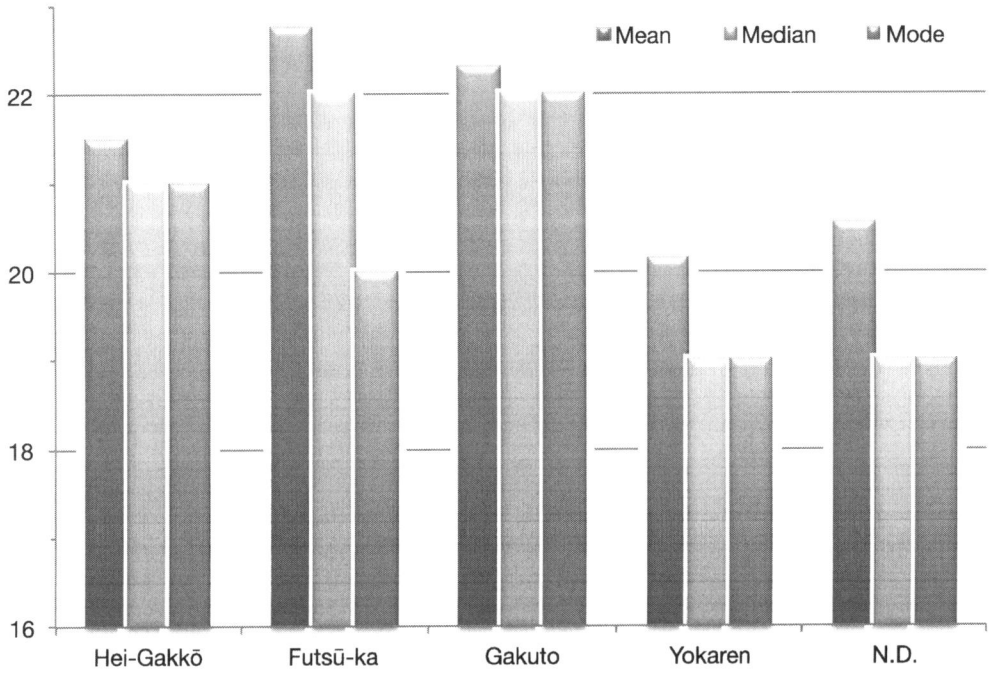

Figure 4 Age distribution by educational background
Source: Author

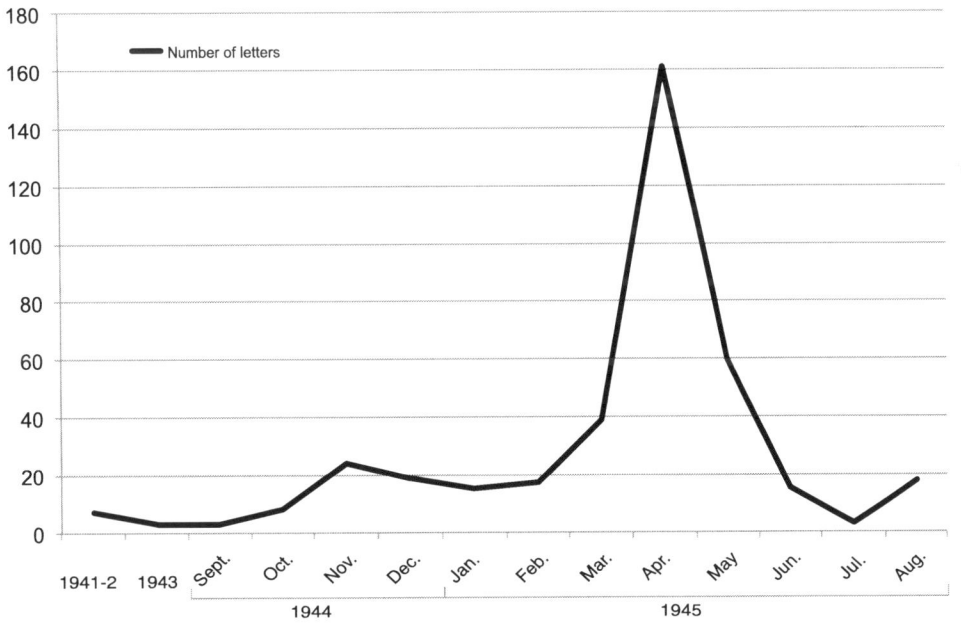

Figure 5 The number of missives written over a time period
Source: Author

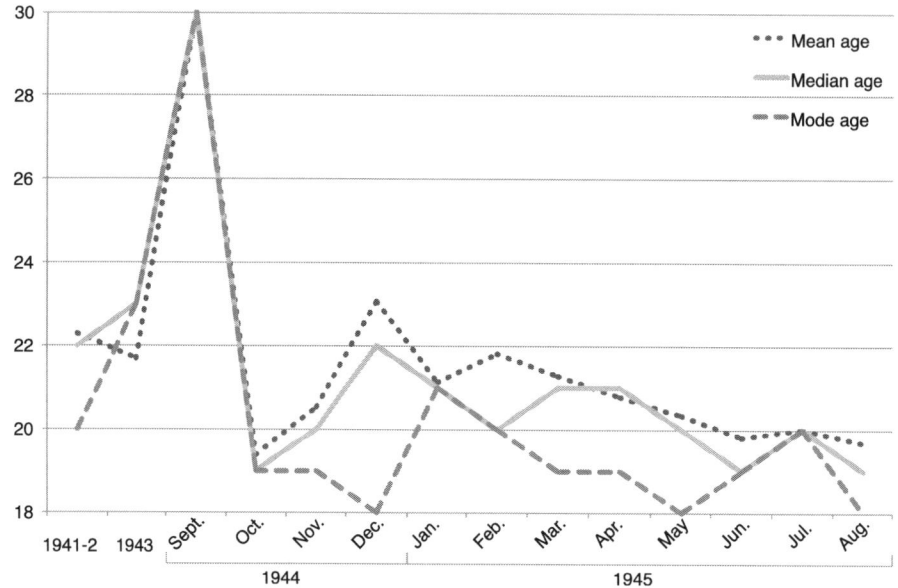

Figure 6 Age distribution of the writers during the high production period
Source: Author

3. Religious affiliation

The families of the Kamikazes never received their loved ones' remains back home. Many did not even know exactly what happened to them. Therefore, Ichirō Ōmi, a civilian, became a pilgrim, visiting grieving families throughout Japan and paying his respects to the war-dead at their family graves, family shrines and alike. He brought back written memorials and submitted them to the Second Demobilization Ministry, which later became the Ōmi Collection. Around 80 per cent of the Collection's artefacts document the Kamikazes' religious affiliations. The statistics (Figure 7) revealed that the majority of the Kamikazes were Buddhists of various denominations, totalling an astonishing 89.64 per cent. Those listed as Shinto followers made up only 9.2 per cent. Other religions include: Tenri-kyō 0.73 per cent and Christians 0.44 per cent. The results refute Premise 3, strikingly contradicting the general assumption of the Kamikazes' strong religious association with Shintoism, as discussed in Section 2 above. Suggestions for a direct link between the Kamikazes and religious fanaticism in Shintoism no longer holds. Rather, the socio-political and historical background of the religious and cultural syncretism needs to be taken into account (Kuroda et al. 1981).

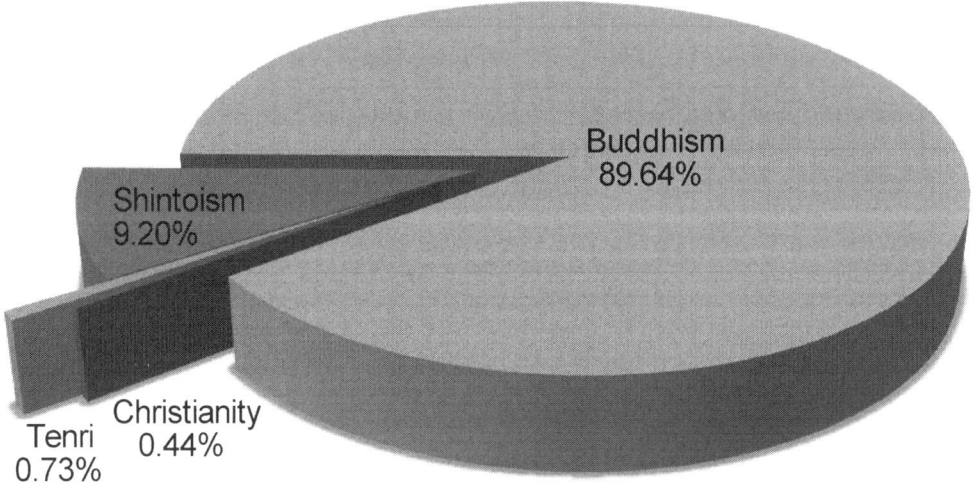

Figure 7 Proportions of religious affiliations
Source: Author

So far, the typical profile of the Kamikaze obtained is: young, 19–20 years old, not a highly-skilled officer, nor a confirmed dogfighter, but a hastily-trained student pilot who died in action, mainly towards the end of the war between October 1944 and August 1945, and who was remembered in Buddhist ceremonial tradition. This is the socio-cognitive context in which qualitative discourse analysis will be conducted below. Before moving on, however, the textual features of the missives are statistically characterized in the next section.

Statistical characterization of the Kamikaze missives home

Overall content. To obtain an overview of the textual and content characteristics, the initial steps include: word extraction, multidimensional scaling (MDS) and word co-occurrence analysis. The texts of the entire sample were first subjected to content and morphological analyses using, respectively, KH Coder (Higuchi 2004) and Mecab (the Nara Institute of Science and Technology), as well as the Kindai corpus of the National Institute for Japanese Language and Linguistics, which covers the Japanese language between the Meiji and early Showa periods. Of all the content words (e.g. nouns, verbs, adjectives, etc.) extracted, those occurring in more than five missives (over one per cent of the total) were marked for categorization. The co-occurrence network yielded the following results. The Japanese words in Figure 8 and the subsequent descriptions below refer directly to the textual contents of the missives that were analysed in the original (and not translated into English) language. Multidimensional scaling (MDS) is a multivariate analysis for the visualization of the underlying structure of a dataset based

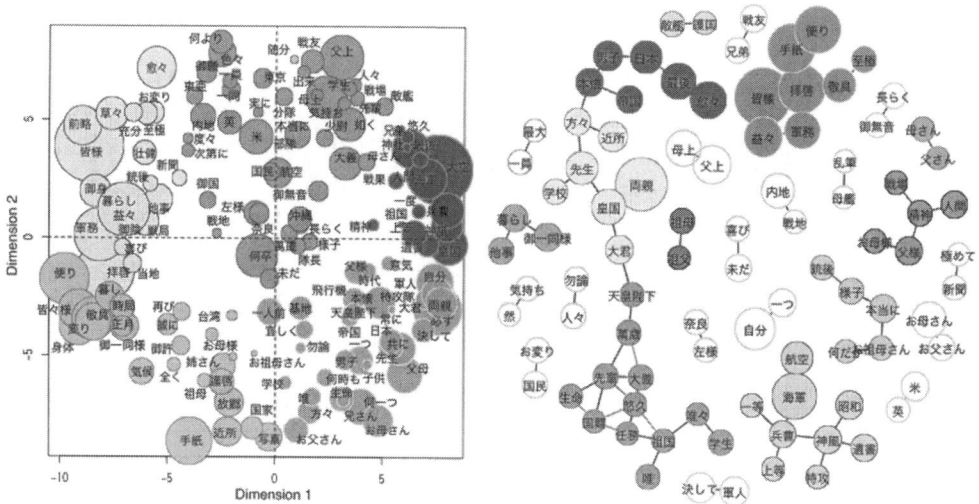

Figure 8 MDS (left) and Collocation network (right). Top seventy-five most-frequently occurring words displayed
Source: Author

on the sample's internal similarity/dissimilarity. Since this technique reduces the multiple dimensions to 2 or 3, the resulting plot is an approximation, but is a useful tool for gaining an overview of the dataset. As shown in Figure 8 (left), the words are plotted over a two-dimensional scattergram. The grey tones differentiate the five different clusters while the size of the bubble shows the magnitude of frequency, i.e. the larger the bubble, the higher the occurrence of the word. The more distant two words are from each other, the more diverging and opposing concepts they express. Hence, the 'Dimensions' 1 and 2, the abscissa and the ordinate of the orthogonal axes, express oppositional trends emerging from the missives. Words further away from the 0 intersection are prominent characterizers of the text in this case.

The various shades differentiate each word cluster with its own internal textual associations. The Kamikaze missives display several semantically distinct groups of associated words. For example, 'family, family-nation (両親, 祖国, 故郷)', 'obligation-responsibility and autonomous decision-making (軍務, 任務, 本懐)', and 'concerns for the family's well-being (暮し, 身体)'. MDS in this study returned a somewhat crowded plot. Even though the analysis reduced the dimensions to two, its interpretation was still not self-evident. Reducing the number of words by raising the threshold occurrence value (e.g., ten times instead of five) is not ideal here either, as it may result in cutting out some important words. Hence, a co-occurrence network analysis (on the right) was performed to complement the MDS. This technique not only classifies the words into 'subgraphs' but also displays the magnitude of occurrence by the bubble size and the strength of the relationship between words as indicated by the 'edges (lines between the bubbles)'. Notably, '大君 (overlord)' in the semantic group 'social system', indicated by the group of white bubbles and '天皇陛下 (your majesty the emperor)' in the semantic group 'empire', in light grey, are the 'nodes' to connect these word groups. This means these 'nodes' create associations of meanings between the groups: they are always used together. However, they are small in size, indicating that they do not appear frequently in the missives. In summary, these word groups referring to the imperial and social systems are most likely parts of formulaic fixed expressions, rather than forming the core message of the missives.

The data revealed surprising facts. Premises 1–4, based on the discussions in section 2, lead us to expect the Kamikaze missives to present 'aggression towards the enemy or the neighbouring lands' or 'fanatic religious zeal'. However, words of hatred and anger (e.g. 憎い、怒り) and murderous intention (e.g. 殺す) were almost totally absent. Expressions of massacre such as 'eliminate, decimate, exterminate (抹殺、殺戮、撲滅)' against other humans were also absent. One notable exception concerns the word 'kill (殺) in 必殺 (sure-death), a figurative expression of maximum impact equivalent to English adjectives such as shattering, knockout, killer, lethal, and alike. Similarly, negative or belligerent action verbs and adjectives of anti-social emotions were almost totally absent in the texts and, on the few occasions they do occur, they refer to the destruction of military vessels, machines, weapons, and institutional systems (特攻、撃沈), not humans. Strikingly, the notion of 'enemy' lacks specification or the naming of the opponent. In fact, no word or morpheme related to imperialism or militarism figures among the top twenty. The first occurrence of a militaristic word, 海軍 (navy), ranks below the fortieth. When military items do appear they come in a formulaic expression and lack variety, being limited to a handful of verbs such as 突撃する 'charge', 撃沈する 'attack to cause sinking', and their nominal variations. Concerning their opponents, less than one per cent of the missives mentioned the US and the UK and those that did, did so exclusively in the context of self-defence and protection of the families in the hometowns. There was no mention of China. The Philippines and Taiwan are mentioned as battle locations only, while base locations were blanked as '〇〇', obviously to conceal where military actions were taking place. Regarding religion, there was no occurrence of words meaning 'death in the faith/believe in Shintoism' but, just occasionally, some letters mention belief in a Buddhist monk, e.g. Nichiren, while others expressed the hope of reaching nirvana in Buddha's compassion. Yasukuni and its euphemistic name, Kudan, were referred to as a 'memorial' to replace a proper gravestone, where the family could visit. In short, the top forty words are related to the notion of family and their members, indicating that the Kamikaze pilots primarily wrote about their relationship with family members, their health and well-being, before their own impending death. Surprisingly, this empirical result refutes Premises 2, 3, 4(a) and 4(b), but it may not be that surprising, given their educational context as discussed in Section 4 below.

Prominent concepts. To investigate the overall features of the missives and how the Kamikazes represented themselves in their own words, associative relations between the subsets of semantic groups within the texts need to be studied. First, 340 different frequently-occurring content words were categorized into 18 subsets according to their semantic categories as follows. (1) Shintoism (神道); (2) imperial expressions (天皇); (3) imperial military expressions (皇軍); (4) military expressions used in their social environment (環境); (5) educational expressions (教育); (6) enemy (敵); (7) conditions of the time (時勢); (8) mission, responsibility (使命); (9) life (生命); (10) emotions (感情); (11) nature and the homeland (自然); (12) ideal youth (理想); (13) family (家族); (14) hometown community (出身); (15) concerns for the addressees' well-being (安否); (16) subjective judgement and perception (主観); (17) self-first person pronoun and associated linguistic items (自己); and (18) letter-writing expressions (手紙).

For each of the eighteen subsets, the number of words composing the relevant subset was counted, then the sum of the occurrences was normalized by dividing it by the number of words composing the subset. The values thus obtained were used as variables.

The histogram in Figure 9 shows the normalized occurrence of each subset demonstrating the incremental pattern from least occurring semantic groups (Shintoism, imperial military) to the most frequently occurring ones (self,

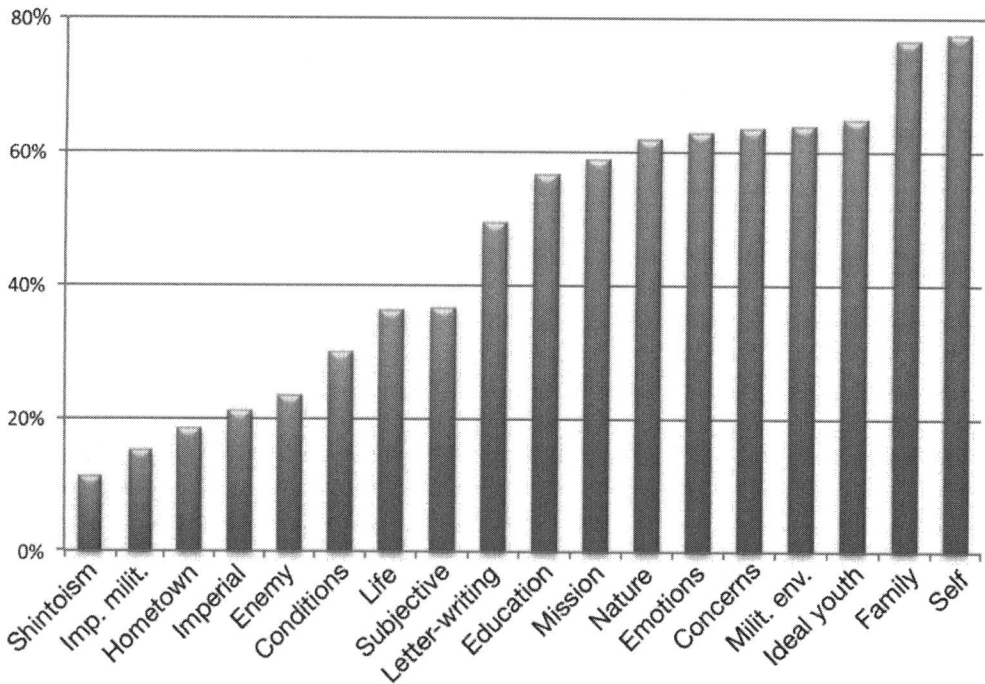

Figure 9 Frequency of occurrences of the semantic groups
Source: Author

Table 2 Variables characterizing 'Self'

---
1. Variables: Emotion
2. Variables: Emotion; Ideal Youth
3. Variables: Emotion; Ideal Youth; Family's Well-being
4. Variables: Emotion; Ideal Youth; Family's Well-being; Mission
5. Variables: Emotion; Ideal Youth; Family's Well-being; Mission; Education
6. Variables: Emotion; Family's Well-being; Ideal Youth; Education; Life; Mission
7. Variables: Emotion; Ideal Youth; Family's Well-being; Education; Life; Nature & Hometown; Mission

---

Source: Author

family). The results reveal that words referring to Shintoism or the emperor have minimal impact, followed by the Empire's military, social standing by birth, the Emperor, and the enemy, refuting premises 3 and 4(a).

Self-representation and associated concepts. Next, to explore the expressions of self-identity by Tokkō-tai members, a multiple regression analysis is used to explain the relationship between the target word group of 'self/identity' and all other sets of words, using multiple linear regression, with the semantic group 'self (first-person linguistic items)' as the response variable and all other sixteen groups as predictors. The results in Table 2 yielded seven models. In each case, variables are given in order of significance, whereby the order changes in models No. 6 and 7.

The alteration in the order of significance is checked further as in Table 3. The line in bold in Model 7 shows the first occurrence of the non-statistically significant parameter 'Mission'. Therefore, we can consider that Models 1–6 only are statistically viable models to explain the contents of the missives in terms of the Kamikaze pilots' self-representation. In Models 1–5, the main components of missives are: Emotion, Ideal Youth, Concern for the family's well-being, and Mission. In models 5–6 Education and Life become more important components than mission.

Table 3 Multiple regression results

Model		Unstandardized B	SE	Standardized β	t-value	p-value	Collinearity Toler.	VIF
1	(Constant)	3.445	0.276		12.471	0.000		
	Emotion	2.025	0.121	0.647	16.755	0.000	1.000	1.000
2	(Constant)	2.711	0.278		9.753	0.000		
	Emotion	1.406	0.142	0.449	9.935	0.000	0.643	1.556
	Ideal youth	0.928	0.127	0.331	7.322	0.000	0.643	1.556
3	(Constant)	2.233	0.287		7.781	0.000		
	Emotion	1.242	0.141	0.397	8.785	0.000	0.607	1.647
	Ideal youth	0.778	0.127	0.278	6.133	0.000	0.605	1.652
	Concern	0.670	0.136	0.197	4.918	0.000	0.770	1.298

(continued)

Table 3 (Continued)

Model		Unstandardized B	SE	Standardized β	t-value	p-value	Collinearity Toler.	VIF
4	(Constant)	1.858	0.290		6.410	0.000		
	Emotion	1.070	0.142	0.342	7.531	0.000	0.569	1.758
	Ideal youth	0.741	0.124	0.265	5.997	0.000	0.603	1.658
	Concern	0.646	0.133	0.191	4.879	0.000	0.769	1.300
	Mission	0.626	0.130	0.178	4.805	0.000	0.858	1.166
5	(Constant)	1.789	0.288		6.218	0.000		
	Emotion	0.926	0.148	0.296	6.237	0.000	0.510	1.960
	Ideal youth	0.641	0.127	0.229	5.061	0.000	0.562	1.779
	Concern	0.677	0.132	0.200	5.147	0.000	0.765	1.308
	Mission	0.523	0.133	0.149	3.922	0.000	0.802	1.247
	Education	0.455	0.150	0.133	3.025	0.003	0.596	1.678
6	(Constant)	1.757	0.286		6.150	0.000		
	Emotion	0.883	0.148	0.282	5.953	0.000	0.504	1.985
	Ideal youth	0.619	0.126	0.221	4.915	0.000	0.560	1.787
	Concern	0.698	0.131	0.206	5.342	0.000	0.762	1.313
	Mission	**0.368**	0.145	**0.104**	**2.544**	0.011	0.671	1.490
	Education	0.413	0.150	0.121	2.756	0.006	0.589	1.697
	Life	0.630	0.237	0.108	2.655	0.008	0.689	1.452
7	(Constant)	1.638	0.288		5.681	0.000		
	Emotion	0.790	0.152	0.253	5.185	0.000	0.471	2.122
	Ideal youth	0.629	0.125	0.225	5.023	0.000	0.559	1.789
	Concern	0.640	0.132	0.189	4.844	0.000	0.736	1.358
	Mission	**0.281**	0.148	**0.080**	**1.895**	**0.059**	0.631	1.585
	Education	0.419	0.149	0.122	2.812	0.005	0.589	1.697
	Life	0.623	0.236	0.106	2.641	0.009	0.688	1.453
	Nature	0.296	0.124	0.095	2.392	0.017	0.705	1.418

Source: Author

As above, the pattern of the Kamikaze's self-representation in their first-person discourse has emerged and is mainly characterized by their emotional expressions, concerns for the image of an ideal youth as well as for the well-being of their family. In addition, their responsibility, obligations and missions combined with education and training, issues of life and poetic images of nature and the homeland were strongly associated with their patterns of self-representation. Hence, Premise 4(c) was refuted. We will next explore qualitatively how such patterns might be interpreted in second and third-person Kamikaze discourse.

Contextualizing the 'Kamikaze' discourse

The features of the Kamikaze texts derived from the statistical results are further examined qualitatively using the framework of Discourse Historical Approach

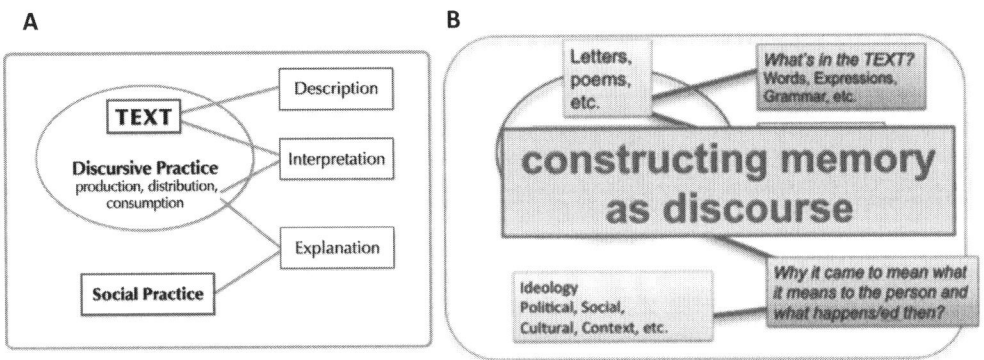

Figure 10 CDA Framework. A B.
Sources: A: Based on Fairclough (1992, p. 73; and 1995, p. 98). B: by the author

within Critical Discourse Analysis (DHA-CDA) (Reisigl and Wodak 2009). CDA operates on three levels of analysis: the discourse text, discursive practice (of production, distribution, consumption), and the social practice-context in which the discourse is found. Figure 10 is a schematic representation of this concept adapted from Fairclough (1992) on the left and its adaptive model for this study on the right.

The three levels consist of the Kamikaze missives home (text), their linguistic contexts (the discursive practice) within the relevant co-texts such as education/training policies, etc. and the Kamikaze's social conditions at the time (social practice). These levels of information interact with each other (van Dijk 2003, p. 354) through the interpretation and communication of the text by people (social actors) and their socio-cognitive representations (SCR) of the text with their 'beliefs and/or knowledge, including second-hand knowledge gained through media consumption, the norms and values held by members of a discourse community, the attitudes and expectations deriving from the combination of beliefs/knowledge, on the one hand, and norms and values, on the other, and the emotions that accrue to all of these elements' (Koller 2012, p. 20). Therefore, the interpretation and consumption of the Kamikazes' discourse by anyone other than the Kamikaze themselves is biased by that person's personal interpretation and agenda. For example, a second person (by referring to the Kamikazes as 'you' in an interpersonal narrative, whether by their relatives in recollection or an empathizing stranger) or a third person (as in academic prose, media, etc.) discourse on the Kamikaze memories frequently refers to topics or subtopics of other discourses, such as the Second World War or the 'zero' fighter plane, or, depending on the socio-political 'frame' of the author, the topic branches out to a variety of war-related issues. Since 'discourses are open and often hybrid; new sub-topics can be created at many points' (Reisigl and Wodak 2009, p. 90), associations between related discourses reinforce the creation of networks of SCRs and, in turn, a preferred interpretation of the discourse of Kamikaze memory may be disseminated through the association of topical concepts as well as the assimilation of the discourse in individuals' comprehension and reproduction of shared discourses. Eventually, this may lead to hegemony of a particular collective memory. We will use the shorthand 'assimilation-association model of discourse transfer' (v.d. Does-Ishikawa 2013) hereon to refer to this process.

At the root of association-assimilation is the original text, whose statistical characterization pointed to the significance of the 'emotive' elements in the Kamikaze missives. Contrary to Premises 1–4 above, these youths expressed their thoughts candidly and logically. Their writings display anguish, desires and doubts, among other natural emotions. Many letters mention conflicting feelings about friendships and romantic relationships. Some voice doubts about their own decision to carry out the mission, but such doubts are typically followed by expressions of reasoning, self-assurance, and self-encouragement. The following is one such example.

> Dear Mother, I have kept contacts with Mr. S— and his family just as it used to be before I joined the Navy. I visited them whenever I was in Tokyo and they fed and treated me so well. Please would you thank them well on my behalf? His daughter is shy, but a lovely girl as you can see in the enclosed photograph. However, it was good that I controlled myself and nothing has happened between us. Only that she may be hoping that one day we will… which thought grips me, but nothing can be done now. She will come to understand my heart one day. Now there is nothing but the good cause before me. Tonight, I am cleansed and in peace in the moonlight. It's for the family, for the Master… Please send everyone my best wishes. I will do it well. I will do it honorably. (Author SI)[5]

The 'spiritual purity' discourse is there, but not in relation to imperialism or militarism. 'Purity' is not referred to substantially in a physical sense but predominantly in the context of 'sincerity' in human relationships expressed in a lyrical discourse (Section 4 below). No clear definition or description of the enemy is found above, but instead only a depiction of an unknown force that threatens 'home and family'. The following example depicts empathy or compassion towards the people of the unknown enemy land. The Kamikaze youth is emotionally troubled, but encourages himself, reminding himself of the duty and the debt of love to his family-nation.

> From the windows of my plane I look to the Imperial land and people that have given me abundant love all along. As I call Banzai[6] praying for victory, my thoughts go to those called 'the enemy' – I imagine the beauty of the land and faces of the people of the enemy nation. Tears well up and I dab my eyes, but I must stand firm in my conviction. I tell myself that there is no other way but to crash into the enemy. (Author MM)[7]

The authenticity of the above words is not in doubt, as the two letters were found in their original state in the envelopes when the analyst consulted the collection, witnessed by two other researchers. Many such examples point to a particular psychological feature: the Kamikazes were in anguish, but they nonetheless chose to go for two reasons: they considered themselves to be 'the chosen ones' and no alternative was possible, otherwise their treasured home would be lost, and with it their identity. It is not hatred of the enemy that propelled the youth to war, but 'the willingness to die in the cause of the homeland' which 'precedes a motive to kill', and with 'great pride in that land' the youth believes that it is 'important for me to serve my country' (Billig 1995, p. 38).

Educational, cultural, and socio-historical contexts

The evidence from this empirical study is compelling: the missives demonstrated how each one of the Tokkō-tai youth, faced with the order to sortie, wrestled with it, considered it, and came to a decision to obey before making their final flight. They were also well educated. The high standard of literacy in the Kamikaze writings across the Ōmi collection points to a highly-effective education system. Indeed, education combined with the sense of mission and images of ideal youth characterized their self-representation patterns. Therefore, we will next explore how the educational background of the Kamikazes may relate to their decision-making processes.

Aspiring to assimilate Western imperial educational models, the Empire of Japan had built what was, for that time, an advanced system with regards to equity and inclusion, albeit superficially. It was a public education system, offered to all pupils, regardless of their socio-economic background. At elementary level the attendance rate exceeded 90 per cent (Ministry of Education White Paper 1981). The missives attest to a high literacy level across all pilots, with a standardized vocabulary, structure, and literary style, but, crucially, their education lacked a global view of citizenship, but was rich in its combination of ideologies.

For the most part, imperial Japanese ideological education was implemented systematically in schools nationwide through the daily drilling exercises of singing songs from state-endorsed songbooks. The aim was to create a sense of solidarity and 'belonging' through the act of singing in unison as noted by Anderson (1991):

> Take national anthems, ... No matter how banal the words and mediocre the tunes, there is in this singing a moment of simultaneity. At precisely such moments, people wholly unknown to each other utter the same verses to the same melody... for the echoed physical realisation of the imagined community.... How selfless this unisonance feels! ... Nothing connects us all but imagined sound.

The 'visceral experience' (Sakamoto 2014) invoked when reading the missives at the Yūshūkan may be partially due to the lyrical quality of the discourse produced by this generation.

The education system prepared children to accept the similarly-themed ideological propaganda spread through the media and a variety of entertainments outside school. The songbooks underwent transitions through four ideological stages, marked by their dates of publications (van der Does-Ishikawa 2013), each stage having its own predominant ideological feature: direct imperialism and state as well as nation-oriented nationalism in Period 1 (1881–1909); direct militarism and indirect nation-oriented nationalism in Period 2 (1910–1930); long, lyrical texts imbued with nation-oriented nationalism, indirect militarism and imperialism in Period 3 (1931–1940); and short, heavily-contextualized texts depicting indirect militarism and ultra-nationalism in Period 4 (1941–1945).

At the time of their deaths Tokkō-tai youths were aged between 15 and 26, and the majority attended elementary school during the early part of the 1930s (Period 3). This was a period of prolonged recession, starting with the 1930 financial crisis followed by civil unrest, prompting the government to tighten control on the society. The 1930s' Jinjō-shōgakkō school system placed special emphasis on the students' ability to appreciate lyricism in literature, combined with nationalist sentiments and the belief in the imperial holiness to which his majesty's subjects take part as a family-nation (Karasawa 1956, Kurokawa 2007). This period nurtured the spirit of spontaneous participation in good causes and independent decision-making as well as acute emotional responses to ethical and cultural aesthetics, combined with an appreciation for imperialist militarism and nationalism. First, children were taught to identify with the family-nation. Secondly, censorship of educational materials resulted in biased information input, nurturing a skewed world view and fear of unknown outsiders. Thirdly, action based on autonomous decision-making was encouraged. Thus, the obligation to 'protect' the family-nation should be an autonomous decision, based not on blind-belief, but on reasoning and free-will. This characteristic was attested to in the missives (see Figure 9 and Table 2). Loyalty to the nation was justified by the doctrine of the imperial family-nation taught in history, geography, language, ethics and other classes by way of integrated inter-curricular teaching. An example of this is shown by the use of the twelfth-century 'Kamikaze' legend (Section 2) read, taught and sung in national language, history, geography, and music lessons. As a result of this education, the Tokkō-tai youth considered themselves to be a self-defence team, pitched against mysterious enemies posing a threat to their homes. This self-image contrasts with the aggressive portrayal of the Kamikazes in today's internet memes or the images associated with Ei-Rei (lit. Significant Spirit, i.e. spirit of the war-dead). So, if not directly from the Kamikaze's self-representation, where does their gallant image come from? The following children's song may hold the key to the answer.

EXCAVATING THE POWER OF MEMORY IN JAPAN

1. 一挙にくだけ、敵主力。 待ちしはこの日、この時と。

Smash the enemy's capital ship at a blow. Today, this moment has been long awaited.

怒濤の 底を 矢のごとく、死地に乗り入る、艇五隻。

From the bottom of the raging billow, five ships came to meet their end.

2. 朝風切りて、友軍機。おそふと見るや、もろともに

Cutting the morning breeze, our force flies. Give no time to the enemy to attack our comrades.

巨艦の列へ射て放つ、魚雷に高し、波がしら。

Open fire on the line of the enemy's gigantic ships. At the explosion of our torpedo a wave crest rises high.

5. ああ、大東亜聖戦に、みづくかばねと誓ひつつ、

Ah, heroes of the Greater East Asian Holy War! Vowing before the Emperor to dedicate their lives to this sacred mission,

さきがけ散りし、若櫻。仰げ、特別攻撃隊。

The young cherry blossoms have gone to lead the way. Let us venerate our 'Special Attack Unit (Kamikaze)

The above are excerpts from the song called *Tokubetsu kōgekitai* from the fifth grade state-endorsed songbook. This would have been sung frequently, nationwide during 1941–1945, at the *Kokumin-gakkō* primary schools, established by the enactment of the 1941 People's School Law. Japan had been at war with China since 1937 and in 1941 entered into the Pacific War (WWII). In a desperate attempt to change the losing course of the war, the 'Thought War (*shisōsen*)' strategy was adopted by the educationists for mobilizing all sections of society and 'unifying the battlefront with the home front' (Kushner 2006, p. 6). This also built on the nationalistic sentiment of a unified Japan that had emerged during the time of the Russo-Japanese War (1904–1905) (Shimazu 2009) and which continued to dominate the society's psyche until its defeat in 1945. Wars were fought for 'imperial' Japan; citizens died the 'honourable deaths' of imperial subjects (Shimazu 2009, pp. 98–99). Under the hegemony of *Kōkoku-shugi* (imperial-nationalism) children at school in Period 4, like their Period 3 predecessors, were imbued with the virtue of individual sacrifice for the sake of the family or the greater good through the systematic, inter-curricular re-enforcement of learning and singing about concepts of the combined ideologies of Imperialism, Militarism, and Ultra-nationalism (Kurokawa 2007, Imagawa and Murai 2013).

The song describes Tokkō-tai in the second- or third-person perspective in declarative sentences. It narrates the action scenes in the third-person voice, while imperative sentences (e.g. Go, Attack, etc.) adopt the second-person perspective, enhancing the sense of immediacy and involvement. This style and perspective closely resembles that of the discourse in exhibitions and publications of war museums, whereby, except for the artefacts of the Kamikaze soldiers themselves, most items (memoirs, obituaries, epitaphs, recollections) are described in the second- or third-person from the perspectives of families and friends, as well as their peers, who were a little younger than Kamikaze pilots. These are the Period 4 generation who worked hard to keep the Kamikaze memory alive. In a style similar to the song above, they have narrated it from a third-person perspective, sometimes shifting into the second-person, addressing the Kamikaze youths as if they were in front of their very eyes. These discourse patterns have established themselves as a genre and been carried on by the later generations, some of whom are visitors to these museums. Thus, in the visitors' books of war museums, one can find messages that read: 'Thank you for giving your precious life to protect our nation. Without you, I would not be here'. Professional domestic writers have adopted a similar discourse style, disseminating it through various media outputs. Thus, as described in the assimilation-association model of discourse transfer, the empathic discourse pattern has come to permeate the mainstream domestic memory of the Kamikaze. Likewise, the Kamikaze's presumed identities have originated in the recollections of those who were close to them, and that was partially based on the self-image that the Kamikazes represented in their missives home and also partially on the popular discourse of the contemporaneous propaganda being circulated during this period, adding to the gallant public image of the Tokkō-tai, which was then immortalized by the later generations' second and third-person discourse of songs and exhibitions. Thus, a gap emerged between the ascribed images and identities of the Kamikaze in collective and individual memories on one hand, and the self-representation produced by the Kamikaze pilots themselves in their writing, on the other.

Conclusion: the uncertain future of recycled memory and Kamikaze identity

The self-representations of the Kamikazes depicted in their missives turned out to be both unique and universal, unified and diverse, all at the same time. They aspired to adopt the public image of a hero, who gives his life to shield the oppressed and persecuted from harm and that is how they ask the readers to remember them, while their words sometimes betray their vulnerability through the discourse markers of suppressed fear, doubt, innocence and desire.

The main features of the missives are found to revolve around self-identity and family/home. They are associated with subthemes consisting of: public 'ideal' image construction, self-assurance and confirmation of one's mission and decisions in life, attempts to suppress emotions, all of which are contextualized within the environment of 'learning and training'. The imagery of '*furusato*', etched into the Kamikaze pilots' minds through a variety of Period 3 educational inputs is most closely associated with their self-identity. This, in combination with the frequent reference to 'learning' in their missives, points to the fact that they spent the entire period of their formative years learning to make autonomous decisions to contribute to society, 'the big family', to which they belonged, even at the cost of their own lives, for the reward that is the eternal honour and membership in the precious community that nurtured them and will never let them down. So they were taught.

Predominantly, the missives are the recordings of a young life, a life still in the process of constructing its self-identity within the circumstances of war, longing for assurance and acceptance by his home-community, trying to encourage the readers and himself alike, sometimes taking recourse to exaggeration, creating triumphant stories of events experienced or heard second-hand. He does so by writing a message to the members of his community, telling them how he would like to be remembered, but it is more of a monologue, or even verbal graffiti when impressionistically expressed. Either way, the act of writing serves to give self-assurance about a life that still exists, but is soon to be lost. The public self-image in the missives is the image of an ordinary youth who displays extraordinary courage under terrible circumstances. This can resonate with today's young generation through empathy, and the image of the suffering hero can translate into a variety of other cultures and situations, too. On the other hand, where affinity is absent it could also be tremendously repelling. Such universal reference may explain the popularity of recycled Kamikaze memories in the social media. The danger is in our emphasizing this public identity alone without the whole picture, which has hitherto been undisclosed. The Kamikazes' inner turmoil, doubts, pains and losses were, until now, only witnessed by those who knew them in person or by those who had access to their self-representations.

This study of authentic Kamikaze missives evidenced a striking scarcity of clear definitions of the 'enemy' and expressions of hatred in the Kamikaze discourse. These results as a historical fact, contrast starkly with many of the modern internet references to the Kamikaze, where aggression against a well-defined enemy in a conflict is the theme. While individual memories tend to focus more on human relationships and the missives discuss suicide as the last-resort, the collective memories focus on the conflict, as in the case of the comparison of the Kamikaze with jihadists (Gupta and Mundra 2005, Küntzel 2007, Moghadam 2008). Where the Kamikazes' individual memories have become subsumed into collective memories and in the absence of the 'voice of the remembered', the original substance begins to fade and is replaced by third-party interpretations. These recycled memories engender limitless versions of presumed Kamikaze identities, as discussed in Section 2, developing in new, uncertain directions. Considering the far-reaching effects of the internet, evidence-based re-examination of documentation and the dissemination of historical facts appear more urgent than ever.

Witnesses of the original Kamikaze sources are advanced in age. In fear of domestic and international controversy, the original 'unedited' writings of the Tokkō-tai are fast disappearing. Soon all will be lost except for the selected theme-based museum exhibitions. Facts that do not fit within a prescribed narrative framework will continue to be edited out (Hodgins 2004, p. 101). Then, one day, the Kamikaze's words will no longer be a memory, but will become an amplified legend in danger of abuse by those furthering anti-social causes or political divisions. It is in this context that this study calls for the preservation of the sources and further large-scale empirical study of the missives in order to enrich the existing contested memories of the Kamikaze and Tokkō-tai youth by studying the mind landscape of the youth in a given sociopolitical context, whereby their ultimate decisions were made. How was the concept of 'undefined enemy', or 'ever-present outside threat' (Dower 2012, p. 53), acquired and interpreted by them? How did such a concept drive them into the war? How can we prevent repeating the same mistake again in the future? These are the questions implicitly and explicitly addressed by the Tokkō-tai survivors, who are confronting the past by leaving testimonies in the manner similar to the '*kataribe* (A-bomb witnesses)' in Hiroshima and Nagasaki. The true drive for these quiet campaigns are 'for peace' at the human level, regardless of the layers of discourse of their 'supposed political intentions'. As evidenced in Hook (1996, pp. 160–179) attempts to keep the Hiroshima/Nagasaki memory alive have had an impact on the public's pacifist, anti-nuclear, domestic peace discourse that crossed national borders to stimulate international debate, and the same potential is witnessed with the Kamikaze missives, whenever read with empathy.

In the Japanese language, 'memory' has a life, and 'wind' is associated with life's destiny (Bulian, this issue). When a memory becomes irrelevant and forgotten we say 'memory has wind-ified (*fūka*: weathered, disintegrated, and gone with the wind)' just as flesh returns to dust. Yet, when the time comes, memory can be 'resurrected (*kioku ga yomigaeru*)' and 'summoned (*kioku wo yobiokosu*)' back from a 'distant place (*kioku no kanata*)' to face the unresolved past and become whole again. As we face the true identity of Tokkō-tai, the missives will act as our go-between.

Acknowledgements

I am deeply grateful to the families of the Tokkō-tai, the Yamato Museum, and to the officers at the JMSDF First Service School for allowing me to access the missives and for providing invaluable information for this research. I would also like to thank Professor Glenn Hook for his guidance, which enabled me to carry out this ambitious project. My heartfelt thanks also go to Professor Andre Rieu, Dr Kerstin Lukner, Dr Giovanni Bulian, and Dr Takashi Suzuki for their expert advice and critical reading and to Ms Claire McAuley and Dr Thomas McAuley for their insightful advice on language, music, and poetry.

This work was supported by the Great Britain Sasakawa Foundation Grant, No. 4728.

Disclosure statement

No potential conflict of interest was reported by the author.

Notes

1. The author thanks Keep Calm Network Ltd. for permission to use the image.
2. お母さん、、、私も願叶って出撃出来る様になりました これが最後です、、、何処に居ても お母さんの事は忘れたことはありません、、、隊長よりの言が耳の底に残って居ります、、『、、、国家の興亡を一身に受けて戦ふ、、、』と、、、お母さん 喜んで下さい 私もやっと一人前の人間になれる時が来たのです、、、私の忘れられぬ様に私はいつもお母さんの心の中に咲いて居ることと思ひます、自分も面白く愉快な人間だったと想って居ります、、、お母さん 優しい笑顔を心の中に画いて敵艦に突入します、、、
3. **Goodnight Saigon**
Words and Music by Billy Joel
Copyright © 1981 JOELSONGS
All Rights Administered by ALMO MUSIC CORP.
All Rights Reserved
Used by Permission
Reprinted by Permission of Hal Leonard Corporation
(The author thanks Mr. Billy Joel represented by Ms. N. Cherwin at Hal Leonard Corporation for the permission to reprint his lyric.)
4. 'I See Fire' Words and Music by Ed Sheeran © 2013, Reproduced by permission of United Lion Music/ Sony/ATV Music Publishing Ltd, London W1F 9LD.
(The author thanks Mr. Ed Sheeran represented by Ms. L. Webb at SONY/ATV Music Publishing for the permission to reprint his lyric.)
5. 母上様東京の■■様とは今だに入隊前と同じ様にお付合いをさせて貰っています。東京に出る度に、否、休みの度にお邪魔し御馳走様になりました。よろしくお礼を申して下さい。■■子嬢は母上も写真でみての通りおとなしいいい娘です。でも想ひ切って然も何事も無しに今日まできて本当によかったと思ひます。でも私を将来は、、、と思っていると思うと ■■の想ひもありますが仕方ありません。きっと私の気持ちを何時か分って呉れるでしょう。大義以外の何者も無く情浄ないい気持ちです。 月が照り輝き 家の為君の為。皆様身体に気を付けて下さい。ではしっかりやります。きっと立派にやりますよ。
6. Lit. 'thousands of years (to the Imperial land)!'.
7. 愛機の内より大君の鎮まり居ます御國の愛を拝し奉り候ひて大君の万才と大日本帝国の必勝を祈り候へば髣髴として湧き興る敵國の山河人々の顔唯唯目頭熱くなり候ひて撃砕せずんば止まざるの念を更に固め申し候。

References

Abe, S., 2006. *Utsukushii Kuni E*. Tokyo: Bunshun Shinsho.

Adams, C., 1994. *The Straight Dope*. Available from: http://www.straightdope.com/columns/read/1035/why-did-kamikaze-pilots-wear-helmets [accessed 30 August 2014].

Anderson, B.R.O.G., 1983/1991. (Revised and extended. ed.). *Imagined communities: reflections on the origin and spread of nationalism*. London: Verso.

Asahi-Shimbun, 2014. Asahi-Shimbun Yoron Chōsa: Shusō no Yasukuni Sanpai, Hantai 46%. Asahi Digital. 27 January, 2014 issue. Available from: http://www.asahi.com/articles/ASG1W3TY3G1WUZPS001.html [accessed 30 August, 2014].

Atia, N. and Davies, J., 2010. Nostalgia and the shapes of history: Editorial. *Memory Studies*, 3 (3). Sage, 181–186.

Billig, M., 1995. *Banal nationalism*. London: Sage.

Brown, G., 1995 *Speakers, listeners and communication: explorations in discourse analysis*. Cambridge: CUP.

Buruma, I., 1995. *Wages of guilt: memories of war in Germany and Japan*. New York: Farrar, Straus and Grioux.

Chiran Peace Memorial Museum (2014) '"Chiran kara no Tegami (Chiran Tokkō-Isho)" no UNESCO Sekai Kioku Isan Tōroku wo Mezashite!'. Available from: http://www.chiran-tokkou.jp/news/sekaiisan/ [accessed August 30, 2014].

Guptaa, D.K. and Mundra, K., 2005. Suicide bombing as a strategic weapon: an empirical investigation of Hamas and Islamic Jihad. *Terrorism and Political Violence*, 17 (4), 573–598.

Douglas, B.J. and Marmar C.R., eds., 2002. *Trauma, memory, and dissociation*. 54. Arlington, VA: American Psychiatric Publishing.

Dower, J., 2012. *Ways of forgetting, ways of remembering Japan in the modern world*. New York, London: The New Press.

Fairclough, N., 1989. *Language and power*. London: Longman.

Fairclough, N., 1992. *Critical language awareness*. London: Longman.

Filmore, C.J., 1971. *Santa Cruze lectures on Deixis*. Berkley: University of California.

Focus Online, 2014. 'WM 2014 in Brasilien ReaktionenKroaten-Wut: "Japan-Killer schießt uns in den Rücken"' (13.06.2014, 11:31). Available from: http://www.focus.de/sport/fussball/wm-2014/reaktionen-nach-auftakt-der-wm-2014-in-brasilien-kroaten-wut-japan-killer-schiesst-uns-in-den-ruecken_id_3918125.html [accessed 30 August 2014].

Hartley, L.P. 1953/2004. *The go-between*. London: Penguin Classics.

Havlíček, J., 2009. Religion, politics and national identity in modern Japan: examining the issue of Yasukuni Shrine. *Religio*, XVII (1), 57–74.

Higuchi, K., 2004. Text-gata Data no Keirō-teki Bunseki: Futatsu no approach no shunbetsu to tōgo. *Riron to Hōhō*, 19 (1), Sūri-Shakai-Gakkai, 101–115.

Hodgins, P., 2004. Our haunted present: cultural memory in question. *TOPIA: Canadian Journal of Cultural Studies*, 12, 99–108.

Hook, G.D., 1996. *Militarization and demilitarization in contemporary Japan*. London and New York: Routledge.

Imagawa, K. and Murai, S., 2013. National character building through the song teaching materials of national schools (Kokumin Gakkō) in Japan: a study on the interdisciplinary curriculum during World War II. *Seishin Studies*, Departmental Bulletin Paper 121, Seishin University, 235–268.

Ishiguro, K., 1982. *A pale view of hills*. London: Faber and Faber.

Jeans, B., 2005. Victims or victimizers? Museums, textbooks, and the war debate in contemporary Japan. *The Journal of Military History*, 69 (1), 149–195.

Jimikelso. 2012. *If Kamikaze Pilots Kill Themselves... Why Do They Wear Helmets?*, memecenter. Available from: http://www.memecenter.com/fun/241649/kamikaze [accessed 30 August 2014].

Joel, B., 1981. ALMO MUSIC CORP./ Hal Leonard Corporation. Written and performed by Billy Joel.

Karasawa, T., 1956. *Kyōkasho no Rekishi: Kyōkasho to Nihonjin no Keisei*. Tokyo: Sōbunsha.

Keep Calm Network Ltd. (n.d.) *Keep Calm and Kamikaze*. THE KEEPCALM-O-MATIC. Available from: http://www.keepcalm-o-matic.co.uk/p/keep-calm-and-kamikaze-3/ [accessed 30 August 2014].

Kil, Y.H., 2010. B-29 to Shōtotsushi Senshi… Bunkotsu shite 'Gunshin' toshite Senden. Available from: http://japan.hani.co.kr/arti/politics/4384.html [accessed online August 30, 2014].

Kil, Y.H., 2014. *Nihon Jisatsu Tokkō-tai-Isho UNESCO-Isan Suishin*. Available from: http://japan.hani.co.kr/arti/international/16625.html [accessed August 30, 2014].

Kingston, J., 2007. Awkward talisman: war memory, reconciliation and Yasukuni. *East Asia*, 24(3), 295–418.

Koller, V., 2012. How to analyse collective identity in discourse: textual and contextual parameters. Critical Approaches to Discourse Analysis Across Disciplines, 5 (2), 19–38. Available from: http://cadaad.net/2012_volume_5_issue_2/79-66, [accessed 1 October 2013].

Kuroda, T., Dobbins, J.C., and Gay, S., 1981. Shinto in the history of Japanese religion. *Journal of Japanese Studies*, 7 (1), 1–21.

Kurokawa, T., 2007. Kokumin gakkō kokuminka kokugo no kenkyu: gengo katsudo shugi to gunkoku shugi no sokoku. Doctoral Thesis. Department of Education, Waseda University.

Küntzel, M., 2007. *Jihad and Jew-hatred: Islamism, Nazism and the Roots of 9/11*. New York: TELOS Publishing.

Kushner, B., 2006. *The thought war – Japanese imperial propaganda*. Honolulu: University of Hawaii Press.

Mahmood, M. and Booth, R., 2013. Syrian army may use kamikaze pilots against west, Assad officer claims. *The Guardian*, Wednesday 28 August 2013 19.32 BST. Available from: http://www.theguardian.com/world/2013/aug/28/syrian-army-kamikaze-against-west-assad [accessed 26 September 2014].

Ministry of Education, Culture, Sports, Science and Technology, Japan. 1981. Japan's modern educational system, *White Paper*. Available from: http://www.mext.go.jp/b_menu/hakusho/html/others/detail/1317220.htm [accessed 31 August 2014].

Moghadam, A., 2008. *The globalization of martyrdom: Al Qaeda, Salafi Jihad, and the diffusion of suicide attacks*. Baltimore, MD: The Johns Hopkins University Press.

Nakar, E., 2003. Memories of pilots and planes: World War II in Japanese manga, 1957–1967. *Social Science Japan Journal*, 6 (1), 57–76.

Nishio, M., 1943. Nihongo Sōryokusen Taisei no Juritsu, *Nihongo*. Ichigatsu-gō. Nihongo Kyōiku Shinkō-sha, 20–21.

O'Dwyer, S., 2010. The Yasukuni Shrine and the competing patriotic pasts of East Asia. *History & Memory*, 22 (2), 147–177.

Ogawa, T., 2014. Dai-36-kai, Abe Shusō no Kenpōkan to Rekishi Ninshiki no Mondaiten. *LIBRA*, 14 (5), 52.

Ohnuki-Tierney, E., 2004. *Kamikaze diaries: reflections of Japanese student soldiers*. Chicago, IL: University of Chicago Press.

Okuyama, M., 2009. The Yasukuni Shrine problem in the East Asian context: religion and politics in modern Japan. *Politics and Religion*, 3 (2), 235–251.

Olick, J., 1999. Collective memory: the two cultures. *Sociological Theory*, 17 (3). (Nov., 1999), 333–348.

Press Association. 2010. Sir Alex Ferguson has accused some of Manchester United's rivals of going on a "kamikaze" spending spree. *The Guardian*, Tuesday 17 August 2010 16.14 BST, Available from: http://www.theguardian.com/football/2010/aug/17/alex-ferguson-transer-market-spending [accessed 23 April 2014].

Reisigl, M. and Wodak, R., 2009. The discourse-historical approach (DHA). *In*: R. Wodak and M. Meyer, eds. *Methods of critical discourse analysis*. 2nd ed. London: Sage, 89–121.

Robertson, J., 1988. Furusato Japan: the culture and politics of Nostalgia. *International Journal of Politics, Culture, and Society*, 1 (4) (Summer, 1988). Springer, 494–518.

Sakaguchi, H., 2005. *Nihon no Uso: Kindaika-Shūen to Miraika*. Tokyo: Bungei-sha.

Sakamoto, R., 2014. Mobilizing affect for collective war memory. *Cultural Studies*, 29 (2), 1–27.

Seaton, P., 2007a. *Japan's contested war memories: the 'Memory Rifts' in historical consciousness of World War II*. London: Routledge.

Seaton, P., 2007b. Family, friends and Furusato: "Home" in the formation of Japanese war memories. *The Asia-Pacific Journal: Japan Focus*, 10 July. Available from: http://www.japanfocus.org/-Philip-Seaton/2469/article.html [accessed 30 August 2014].

Sheeran, E., 2013. *I See Fire*. United Lion Music/ Sony/ATV Music Publishing Ltd, London W1F 9LD. Written and performed by Ed Sheeran.

Shimazu, N., 2009. *Japanese society at war: death, memory and the Russo-Japanese War*. Cambridge: CUP.

Soniak, M., 2013. *Why did Kamikaze pilots wear helmets?, mental_floss*. Available from: http://mentalfloss.com/article/26510/why-did-kamikaze-pilots-wear-helmets [accessed 30 August 2014].

Takahashi, T., 2013. Teikoku Kaigun ni okeru Jinji to Kyōiku. Shōwa 16-nen Tōji (Kaisen-chokuzen) no Jin-teki Unyō wo Chūshin ni. *Senshi Kenkyū Nenpō 16, Bōei-Kenkyūjo Sōritsu 60-shūnen Kinen Tokubetsu-gō*; Bōei-Kenkyūjo.

Tanaka, Y., 2005. Japan's Kamikaze pilots and contemporary suicide bombers: war and terror. *The Asia Pacific Journal: Japan Focus*, 25 November. Available from: http://japanfocus.org/-Yuki-TANAKA/1606/article.html [accessed 30 August 2014].

Tokkō-tai Senbotsusha Irei Heiwa Kinen Kyōkai, eds. 2008. *Tokubetsu-Kōgeki-tai Zenshi*. Dai-1-bu: Tokubetsu-Kōgeki-tai 5-tei-ban, Dai-2-bu: Jun-Tokkō Senbotsu-sha Meibo (Dai-2-kantai, Kaiten, Rikugun-Kaijō-Teishin-Sentai-tō-Senbotsu-sha). (PIIF) Tokkō-tai Senbotsu-sha Irei Heiwa-Kinen-Kyōkai) (eds.). Tokyo: Chūō-Insatsu.

Truitt, B., 2015. "Fury Road" revs up the "Mad Max" mythology, *USA Today*, 13 May 2015. Available from: http://www.usatoday.com/story/life/movies/2015/05/12/mad-max-fury-road-characters-vehicles-mythology/27136835/ [accessed 13 May 2015].

van der Does-Ishikawa. 2013. *A Sociolinguistic Analysis of Japanese Children's Official Songbooks 1881-1945: Nurturing an imperial ideology through the manipulation of language*. PhD Dissertation, University of Sheffield.

van Dijk, T., 2003. The discourse-knowledge interface. *In*: G. Weiss and R. Wodak, eds. *Critical discourse analysis*. Theory and Interdisciplinarity. 85-109. Houndmills: Palgrave-Macmillan.

Yanagida, K., 2014. *Boom Sainen 'Reishiki Sentōki' Zōsatsu, Zero kara Tsunagaru Nihon no Sugata*. Available from: http://www.zakzak.co.jp/people/news/20131002/peo1310020734000-n1.htm [accessed 30 August, 2014].

Yoshida, T., 2007. Revising the past, complicating the future: The Yūshūkan war museum in modern Japanese history. *The Asia-Pacific Journal: Japan Focus*. Available from: http://www.japanfocus.org/-takashi-yoshida/2594 [accessed 30 August, 2014].

Yoshida, Y., 2013. *From cultures of war to cultures of peace: war and peace museums in Japan, China, and South Korea*. Portland, ME: MerwinAsia.

Zongduo, W., 2014. Flying in the face of reason, China Daily USA. Available from: http://usa.chinadaily.com.cn/epaper/2014-02-17/content_17287071.htm [accessed 23 April 2014].

Invisible landscapes. Winds, experience and memory in Japanese coastal fishery

GIOVANNI BULIAN

Abstract: Drawing on a series of ethnographic cases of some fishing communities, the article explores the role of meteorological winds in Japanese coastal fisheries. In particular, it is argued that Japanese fishermen's ecological knowledge is strictly connected to memory that coexists with other institutional knowledge, such as meteorology, in a complex scenario of contestation and negotiation. The article stresses also the idea that fishermen's memory is implicitly subversive to the dominant native discourses on knowledge proposed by Japanese folklore studies, focused on its epistemological hierarchization (folk and scientific knowledge), or on the individualization of the intergenerational discrepancies between traditional and contemporary knowledge. It will attempt to show how the method of interpretation traditionally adopted by this academic discipline offers a vision of fishermen's ecological knowledge that is more susceptible to local and static evocations, and which is far from reflecting the complex relationship between coastal fisheries, memory and knowledge.

Introduction

In Japan, the perception of wind assumes an important cultural role because of the geographical position of the archipelago; it is particularly exposed to strong seasonal winds. In coastal fisheries, wind is a natural phenomenon that involves processes of cognition and practical knowledge based on the daily and past experience of those who live in direct contact with the sea. Strictly connected with the fact of operating in a particular environment such as the sea, the possession of information relating to the local environment and climate increases the rate of productivity as well as reflects the relationship between the mode of learning and fishery management, both inextricably linked to certain historical models of social organization and cultural production. Fishermen's ecological knowledge is crucial both to identify a classification of semantic structures of the environment, including landscape perception, as well as to determine the social and economic implications in the competitive strategies of Japanese fishermen.

This article argues that the 'experience of wind' in Japanese coastal fishery still has a practical engagement with the environment and landscape,[1] where the extreme variability of the strength of the winds, their direction and the humidity of the air masses, the eternal interaction between wind and waves, still generate a 'muscular consciousness' (Bachelard 1964, p. 11) among fishermen. This personal and physical experience of the environment is sustained by past and present sensory recollections regarding meteorological agents that produce implicitly a 'working memory' (Rigney 2005, p. 11), 'constructed and reconstructed in public acts of remembrance and evolves according to distinctly cultural mechanism' (Rigney 2005, p. 11).

Memory – as an expression of social thought that presides over the transmission of meaning about fishermen's geographical surroundings – offers a cultural discourse of the experience of generations of fishermen, a 'history from below', that metamorphoses constantly and is thus never rigid or nostalgically 'authentic'. In the first place, it is argued that Japanese fishermen's memory concerning winds is not a static and objectified cultural heritage connected to vernacular traditions passed down by generations of farmers and fishermen, but it is inherently functional, and is continually reshaped by bodily and practical experiences. Consequently, memory and ecological knowledge are configured not as mechanical strategies for affirmation of undisputed cultural values and identities, but as scenarios for discussion, contestation and negotiation between 'voices' (fishermen, meteorologists, academic scholars and other institutional figures) in a complex arena such as the maritime environment.

Second, contestation is stressed particularly by the idea that memory, as a 'living entity', is implicitly subversive of the dominant native discourses on knowledge, focused on its epistemological hierarchization (folk and scientific knowledge), or on the individualization of the intergenerational discrepancies between traditional and contemporary knowledge. In this context, memory concerning fishermen's traditional knowledge is therefore considered an example of 'contested memory', in which 'contested' is interpreted as an epistemological critique of traditional and current thinking that relegates Japanese weather knowledge to folkloric heritage in dissolution or subjugated by hegemonic scientific knowledge (Nomura 1995, Sekiguchi 2000, Nakayama 2009). As will be seen, the hypothesis that the wind is a cultural coordinate along which the Japanese fishermen build in part their local knowledge and their cultural heritage represents a constant that always finds a precise designation in different descriptive and interpretative discourses on fishermen's ecological knowledge. The key idea of this study, which mainly draws on the works of Tim Ingold (2003), is that ecological knowledge and memory constitute a 'processual knowledge', where they make sense just because they are in relation to a particular environment and they are continuously generated and regenerated within the context of practical skills (Ingold 2000, 2003).

Although translating this theoretical approach into specific protocols of ethnographic research in modern Japanese fishery is not straightforward, local knowledge and memory could have a relevant role in strongly localized socio-economic contexts such as fishing communities, which range from a traditional sense of a resource-dependent community with small-scale family-based fisheries, to occupational encoves in industrialized cities. As repositories of traditional knowledge, practical skills, and cooperative fishing techniques, Japanese fishing communities still exhibit a highly nuanced ecological sophistication: fishing strategies, tides and fishing time, ritual cultures, cognitive maps of the sea bed, vernacular nomenclatures of marine flora and fauna, fishermen's practical observations of the weather, the relationship among fishing areas, climatic dynamics of seasons and fishing techniques, to give some examples, represent a body of traditional knowledge and offer a critical supplement to contemporary interdisciplinary scientific understanding of the Japanese maritime environment (Yanagi 2008).

The article has a theoretical introduction on ecological knowledge, using an interdisciplinary and comparative approach in order to explain how fishermen's experience of winds is experiential, embodied in daily practice, and essentially based on an acquisition of knowledge in practice and skill. In contrast to this approach, the third section explains how memory is still conceived in Japanese folklore studies (*minzokugaku*)[2] as a kind of vanishing inheritance, a substance passed down from generation to generation. To recontextualize the contributions made by this academic discipline, in the fourth section, using an ethnohistorical approach, we explain how winds are 'translated' into a vernacular coding system, which highlights the multitude of microclimate nuances and constructs meaningful relationships between linguistic encoding of local winds and practice, in which language is a modality for disclosing practical memory. In the fifth section, the article considers the empirical level of a number of fishing communities located in the Ise Bay area (Kamishima-chō and Kuzaki-chō, Mie prefecture), in order to elaborate how the experience of wind is a shared and negotiated system of subjective meanings informed by the knowledge and memory that local fishermen put into practice. The subsequent section develops the discussion of the previous sections by exploring the symbolic meaning of winds as articulated through a complex system of social and ideational associations with local landscapes, in which local winds (re)create an affective dimension, a physical space made by climatic agents and invested with a 'total' meaning, evocative of a particular social and economic group. It is here argued that Japanese fishermen's knowledge defines the cultural coordinates of what I define 'invisible landscape', where 'landscape' is an anthropological concept identified through theories of cultural practices and environmental perception incorporated through memory. The article concludes with some critical considerations on the possible ways of understanding the continuity of the relationship between memory and ecological knowledge in contemporary Japanese coastal fishery.

The experience of wind

When talking about winds, an implicit recognition exists among Japanese coastal fishermen between cognition, embodied practice and economic production. Tactical knowledge helps mariners and fishermen to understand wind patterns and also reflects other 'meteorological meanings', such as a phenomenological discourse of knowledge of the maritime environment. As an old fisherman from Kamishima-chō (Toba-shi, Mie prefecture) told me during my fieldwork, it is necessary have a good view, intuition and a good technique for a large catch (*tairyō*).[3] Similarly, concepts are expressed by another fisherman, Matsuji Shindo (1907–93), from Mitsu area (Akitsu-chō, Hiroshima prefecture), who wrote several volumes about his experience, in which he often used the following words to describe his job: instinct, thought, practice, reaction, consideration, handle, treat, become familiar, and deal with (get used to) (Shindo 1994, p. 329). According to Matsuji's biography, when he stood on a hill to observe the fishing ground, he clearly 'understood' the condition of the sea not simply by watching the seawater, but by *feeling* the seascape by using all his senses (Shindo 1994). In Japanese coastal fishing, 'feel the wind' (*kaze o kanjiru*) reflects the general discourses of nautical experience in the varying wind and sea conditions as well as the production of practical knowledge concerning small to medium size fishing boats and an understanding of one's meteorological and maritime surroundings.

Theoretical scholarship suggests that the phenomenology of wind is implicitly associated with the notion of 'embodiment' (Csordas 1994),[4] a theme that emerges constantly in discussing issues surrounding the anthopology of the senses (Low and Hsu 2008, p. 9). In terms of human capacity for bodily knowledge, a growing corpus of anthropological literature (Rappaport 1997, Gray 2000, Merleau-Ponty 1945) recognizes bodily human experience as an existential condition in which the body is the source of the subjective and inter-subjective ground of experience, which applies to the culture and experience, that can be understood from the point of view of being-in-the-world (Csordas 1994). From this perspective, wind should ideally provide a phenomenological attempt to combine knowledge and experience. 'Wind can be smelt, heard and felt, if not touched, and its effects are visible', as Elisabeth Hsu and Chris Low pointed out, 'As wind, including smell and sound, sometimes in combination, is often felt but not seen, it is also a readily available causal concept for events that can be felt to occur but are not seen to occur' (Hsu and Low 2008, p. 9).

In the context of the marine environment, bodily experience is connected to nautical and fishing technology, causing a 'cultural shift' to the discourses of the maritime environment's perception. The sea is a 'dangerous and alien environment', James Acheson observes, 'in which man is poorly equipped to survive, [...] a realm that man enters only with the support of artificial devices' (Acheson 1981, p. 276). 'At sea the body is no longer central to perception. The combination of wind and waves takes effect not on the body but on the boat', Jake Phelan states, 'size, depth and distance, position and direction, become relative to the boat, no longer relative to the person. The lived body still perceives, but this experience of the world is mediated through technology' (Phelan 2007 p. 3). According to some of the more common and basic meteorological observation, the perception of the direction and strength of the wind is based on what a boat 'experiences' through the combination of the 'true wind' and wind that occurs due to the forward motion of the boat. Gisli Pállson (1994) states that a boat becomes part of a fisherman's body, a 'bodily extension in quite a literal sense' (Pállson 1994, p. 910), and he re-directs his analytical attention to the fishermen's experiential processes based on fishing technology.

This definition of experience is subtended by a fundamental assumption: a dialectic relationship between the cultural representation of the surrounding environment and the paradigm of being-in-the-world (Csordas 1994), two approaches that are to be understood as dialogic partners. This implies that subjectivity is not a pure expression of the mind, but intentionally mediated by the body, which can also follow paths that do not use semiotic or symbolic representation. In other words, knowledge is not only propositional, but also practical. The importance of the perception of wind, in terms of the effective evaluation of atmospheric signals, then shows that the perceptual knowledge of the environment has always been the key to the practical knowledge of everyday life. In this context, practical knowledge reflects a wide range of interchangeable definitions and concepts according to disciplinary traditions: 'indigenous knowledge' (IK), 'indigenous technical knowledge' (ITK), 'ethnoecology', 'local knowledge', 'folk knowledge', 'traditional knowledge', 'rural people's knowledge', 'traditional ecological knowledge' (TEK), and so on (Ellen and Harris 2000, p. 2). This set of terms is condensed in a series of common characteristics encapsulated into 'indigenous knowledge': an empirical-hypothetical, orally-transmitted knowledge, rooted in a particular place, focused on particular individuals, connected to practical engagement in everyday life, and characteristically situated within broader cultural traditions (Ellen and Harris 2000, pp. 4–5). Although the debate on IK is complex and extensive, in the context of Japanese coastal fisheries, the paradigm of 'traditional ecological knowledge' (Berkes 1999) has been proposed as a way to analyse the cultural practices of coastal fisheries (Wilhelm 2003).

Even if an universally accepted definition remains for the future – both 'tradition' and 'ecological knowledge' being considered academically ambiguous (Berkes 1999, p. 5) – traditional ecological knowledge is generally defined as 'a cumulative body of knowledge, practice and belief, evolving by adaptive

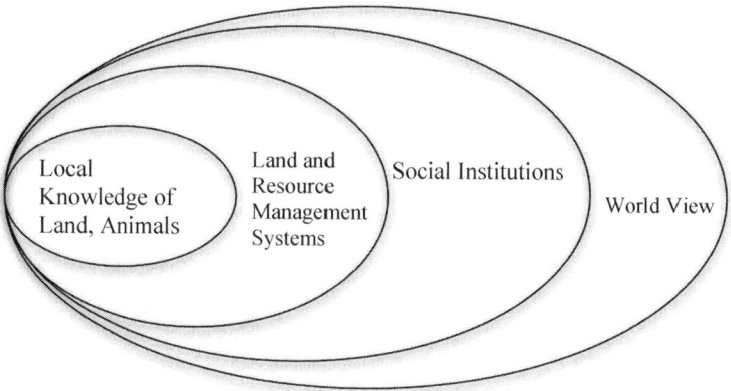

Figure 1 Levels of analysis in traditional ecological knowledge (Berkes 1999, p. 13)

processes and transmitted between generations through cultural transmission, about the relationship of living beings (including the human) between them and with their environment' (Berkes 1999, p. 8). According to Fikret Berkes, this 'knowledge-practice-belief complex' (Berkes 1999, p. 13) is considered at four interrelated levels (see Figure 1). The first level includes local taxonomic knowledge of flora, fauna, soil and landscape. At the second level can be identified the functional relationship between resource management systems and local environmental knowledge. The third level includes social institutions, codes and rules-in-use and, finally, the fourth level is the 'worldview', which shapes environmental perception, comparable to Arne Kalland's 'paradigmatic knowledge' (Kalland 1994, Berkes 1999, p. 14).

Traditional ecological knowledge (TEK) is a 'collaborative concept' (Whyte 2013) that defines the relationship between the human species and the environment in terms of practical, linguistic and perceptual ways. It is defined in science and policy literature as improving cooperative environmental and natural resources management (Berkes and Folke 1998, Nadasdy 1997). However, from a different point of view on the debate of ecological knowledge, this idea that the practitioners' knowledge lies in the accumulations of received mental content (values, rules and representations) for the cultural transmission is essentially a 'genealogical model' (Ingold 2003, p. 307). It is based on 'the idea that the elements that go together to constitute a person are passed down, along one or several lines of descent, from that person's ancestors, independently and in advance of his or her life on the land, in an environment' (Ingold 2003, p. 307). This concept of traditional knowledge, according to Tim Ingold, relegates the environment to a marginal role, a 'backdrop of nature against which a certain way of life is played out' (Ingold 2003, p. 301), suggesting instead 'that the essence of practitioners' environmental knowledge lies in skills, that is in developmentally embodied practices of awareness and response built up through a history of involvement with the land and its inhabitants' (Ingold 2003, p. 301).

These two understandings of ecological knowledge are distinguished by Tim Ingold in two different approaches: 'traditional knowledge in modernist conception' (abbreviated as MTK), embedded in a modernist conception, which is in contrast to what he defines as 'traditional knowledge in local conception' (abbreviated as LTK): 'whereas MTK consists of items of knowledge that are stored in memory, from which they may be accessed and expressed in memory, LTK subsists in practical activities themselves, activities that may also be understood as ways of remembering' (Ingold 2003, p. 308). And finally, the fundamental distinction between MTK and LTK hinges between considering this body of traditional knowledge as a kind of *substance* – in which a human being is considered as a 'container' for intergenerational cultural transmission – or a *process*, in which traditional knowledge is continually reshaped by practical skills (Ingold 2003, p. 308). In other words, '[s]kills are not transmitted from generation to generation', Ingold explains, 'but are regrown in each, incorporated into the *modus operandi* of the developing human organism through training and experience in the performance of particular tasks' (Ingold 2000, p. 5).

In this proposed architecture of cognition and experience, this multilayered relationship between the practice of navigation and memory permits us to understand how knowledge concerning winds accumulated over time could persist among Japanese fishing communities. From this perspective, although no general agreement on the definition of ecological knowledge is yet to be found, the question of a flexible constitution of an operative and skilled knowledge offers, ideally to the context of memory, a strategic role in Japanese nautical culture.

In the next section, the strong intuitive components that characterize this diverse body of knowledge, including the production of memory, offer a broad but also rigid interpretative framework in the field of Japanese folklore studies. The discussion will then examine the main contributions made by this academic discipline in relation to the distinction of ecological knowledge proposed by Ingold (2003). It will attempt to show how the method of interpretation traditionally adopted by Japanese folklore studies generally tends to fall into the category of 'traditional knowledge in modernist conception', a vision of ecological knowledge that is more susceptible to local and static evocations, and which is a long way from reflecting the complex relationship between coastal fisheries, memory and knowledge.

Native discourses on wind

In a more critical and comparative approach, several interpretations of ecological knowledge have been proposed by the subdisciplines of Japanese folklore studies such as *kankyō minzokugaku* ('environment folklore') or *seitai minzokugaku* ('folklore of ecology'), which investigate the relationship between the environment and humans. In Japanese folklore studies, particularly relevant is the study of *nariwai* ('sustenance for living', as fishing and farming activities) or *nariwai fukugō* ('*nariwai* complex'; Nomoto 2008),[5] in which the theoretical analysis of native folklore studies points out key concepts hypothetically similar (but structurally different) to anthropology: *shizen shi* ('instinctive knowledge'), 'the base of life skills, intelligence and sensitivity that you need when you face to nature' (Shinohara 1995, p. 10), and that is a 'notion in contrast to *moji chi* [literal knowledge]. [...]. Non-written information. [...] A synthetic knowledge when facing and observing nature' (Shinohara 1995, p. 10), and could reflect Bourdieu's habitus theory (1990). This practical knowledge – comparable to what Claude Lévi-Strauss described as *science du concret*, and defined in terms of the ability of social action in a given environment – is essentially based on observation, that Shinohara defines as *shintai chi* ('bodily knowledge') (Shinohara 1995).

However, in the internal debates of this discipline, there have been other interpretations over the constitution of ecological knowledge in Japanese culture. One of the most discussed interpretations is the idea formulated by Nomoto that ecological knowledge is a 'pre-established harmony' (Nomoto 1988). Although it has been criticized as a 'reductive argument' focused on a 'primitive and ancient era' (Suga 2001), the interpretation of Nomoto satisfies the 'elegant logic' of the past and contemporary discourses of Japanese folklore studies, generally focused on the lost arcadia and fetishized in the political image of *furusato* (old village, Ivy 1995, Robertson 1998). Since its founder, Kunio Yanagita (1875–1962), Japanese folklore studies have imposed a path of detailed observations of acts, gestures and linguistic expressions, in the urgency to capture the richness and complexity of a disappearing folk heritage. As Kunio Yanagita emphatically wrote: 'When I began to ask questions about local customs and traditions, one old woman burst into tears of joy and exclaimed: "Is the time come when we may tell these *things* [my italics] to strangers who come to inquire?"' (Yanagita 1963, p. 51). These *things* – as Kunio Yanagita reported, as ideally accessible to folklorists thanks to the 'open-hearted old man or woman ready to describe [them]' (Yanagita 1963, p. 51) – are what Nomoto defined as 'treasure', and that Japanese folklorists have a duty to 'hand down' for the future generations (Nomoto 1988). This process of 'traditionalisation of the tradition' is clearly an example of 'traditional knowledge in modernist conception' (Ingold 2003), which is unequivocally located within an ethnic container such as Japanese folk heritage.

According to this perspective, a similar approach has been adopted by folklorist Masanori Nakayama (2009, p. 1) for the study of the winds:

> [...] we are losing such delicacy [wind perception]. It is not proved scientifically either written in historical materials. It will be the role of Japanese folklore to collect our losing senses and record them through oral tradition. We must search oral traditions about wind, and record our sense toward the wind as our

wisdom. Otherwise, such oral traditions and our sense toward the wind may soon disappear completely. The role of Japanese folklore should be to record such traditions and hand them down to the next generation.

Similar understandings of ecological knowledge as 'something that is vanishing' are present not only in the Japanese folklore literature. For example, meteorologist Takeshi Sekiguchi (2000, p. 10) in his introduction of *Kaze no jiten* (*Dictionary of Winds*) writes about the decline of fishermen's wind culture:

> City people have no necessity to distinguish wind directions. Wind is wind. That is all. In fact, even in the weather forecast [...] only people who use wind in their daily life give a name to different winds because wind is their biggest concern. They are fishermen and sailors. There was a saying among them: 'it is hell under a single board at the bottom of a ship' [it is very dangerous and scary to work at sea]. But even in the case of those winds people do not have such fear any more today. Thanks to technological development, a ship became bigger with a motor. Fishing methods have been automated. Their work is much less influenced by the wind today.

Although Sekiguchi's research is based exclusively on surveys and not on ethnographic research, similar complaints are expressed also by folklorists such as Fumitaka Nomura (1995, p. 127), who pointed out the erosion and the marginalization of fishermen's ecological knowledge concerning local and seasonal winds:

> Today, Himawari,[6] a weather satellite, sends us the image of clouds above Japan every hour. [...] Even ordinary people can predict tomorrow's weather from the movement of the clouds sent by Himawari. On the other hand, our ancestors used to read the change of wind, clouds and other natural phenomena to predict weather. It was very important to read the weather for protecting themselves. They did not miss any tiny change of clouds, winds, air, animal behaviour and plants. Wisdom was made with experience and data over a long time, and has been handed down in the form of proverbs. But we are losing such wisdom in modern society with scientific information.

Instead of interpreting 'Himawari culture' as a symbol of hegemonic scientific knowledge, as Japanese folklorists generally suggest, this capital of local knowledge should be considered to be linked to local epistemologies that should be integrated in the 'cultural fabric of thought, discourse and practice' (Hassan 2000, p. 121), in order to negotiate multivalent and shifting meanings. This operation places ecological knowledge and related memories in the everyday world of doing things, related to a given environment in a dynamic operative process. It considers Japanese rural communities not as 'imbued with tradition', but as dynamic entities, which are ready to interact and innovate, suggesting they inhere a complexity that goes far beyond the recording of their transformations over time.

It could be argued that Japanese folklore studies are prey to the opacity of the concept of tradition. This approach is implicitly connected to the critical discourses of the present stagnation of Japanese folklore studies. In this regards, Scott Schnell and Hiroyuki Hashimoto have argued that 'The strategy of addressing each community or geographical area in isolation resulted in masses of descriptive data, but little theory to render the data meaningful or enhance our understanding of the human experience. Thus folklore studies as a whole failed to achieve the kind of theoretical maturity characteristic of the other social sciences' (Schnell and Hashimoto 2003, p. 187). They explained that this course was set after the death of the founder of this discipline (Kunio Yanagita 1875–1962) and that Japanese folklorists nowadays 'have gradually come to recognize the stagnation in their discipline and are presently engaged in a re-examination of their intellectual history in an effort to break the impasse' (Schnell and Hashimoto 2003, p. 188). Japanese folklore might have been able to adapt also to the profound socio-cultural change of Japan, but the sedimentation of simplified use of analytical-descriptive categories and the insistence on a nearly inertial restricted set of theoretical approaches have produced a widespread traditional way of dealing with folk traditions. In addition, Akiko Mori observes that Japanese folklorists are currently doing research on environmental and urban cultures, tourism, cultural heritage, or discrimination, even if such issues are still problematic within the framework of folklore studies (Mori 2014, p. 217). The long shadow of Kunio Yanagita still influences the study of folklore that continues to define itself as *minkan-denshō* (vernacular tradition) as its key concept (Mori 2014, p. 218).

As we will see, this brief critical analysis serves to recontextualize the contributions made by this discipline and to provide the necessary basis for introducing the ethnographic context on the fishermen's ecological knowledge and the role of memory. Therefore, in contiguity with the topics covered in these two sections and to better define what is meant by 'processual knowledge' – to overcome this objectifying interpretation of Japanese folklore studies – in the next sections, we will explain how memory operates and interacts with classification practices of seasonal and local winds.

A meteorological mosaic

In Japan, seasonal winds have an important resonance in climatological terms, because of their geographical position: the great extension in latitude of the archipelago, the proximity to the Eurasian continent, land fragmentation, climatic differences from north to south, influences of surrounding seas and ocean currents, and especially the monsoonal air masses, that dominate the weather conditions throughout southeastern Asia.[7] During the winter months, the prevailing winds are from the northwest, having originated over the cold landmass of eastern

Siberia, while in summer winds blow from the southwest, having originated over tropical seas. The winter and the summer monsoons are not continuous air streams with frequent air interruptions in the seaward flow of polar continental air in winter and the landward flow of tropical-maritime air in summer. In all seasons, one could say, winds blow from several point of the compass.

Historically, Japanese nautical experience had been shaped by frequent non-periodic weather changes during the winter and the summer monsoons. Many historical accounts offer reliable knowledge of the local wind conditions on the coasts: *Senko-Yojutsu* (*Handbook of Navigation*) written by Masafusa Murakami in 1456, provided laws deduced from experiences concerning the wind conditions and topography, describing the monsoon as *banfū* or *ban no kaze* ('turn wind', 'main wind' or 'prevailing wind'; Yoshino 1979, p. 167). *Shinan kōgi* ('A wide sense interpreting of teaching') written by Tei (in 1708), is another interesting description of the relationship between sailing methods and favorable or unfavorable wind conditions (Yoshino 1979, p. 167). The relationship between the circulation regimes of the local winds and topographic settlements was an essential aspect of the sailing culture from the Edo to the Meiji period. Many ports, called *kazemachiko* ('waiting wind port') were strategically built on Ise Shima coasts of the Kii Penisula and on the southern coasts of Izu Penisula, where ships waited for favourable winds (Aono 1938, pp. 234–249; Yoshino 1979, p. 167).

Folk classification of winds in the history of Japanese nautical culture has occupied a central role in dialect investigation and traditional lexicography. Kunio Yanagita, wrote five articles about wind direction in a volume entitled 'Research report of Shusō-gun, Ehime-ken'. In 1935, these articles were published as *Fūikō shiryō* (*Material of Wind Direction Study*) by Dialect Laboratory at Kokugakuin University with two new Yanagita articles: *Tamakaze (2)* and *Sono tsuchi no fūna* (Other wind names) and, in 1942, an enlarged edition was published of Yanagita's research, entitled *Zōho fūikō shiryō* (*Enlarged Material of Wind Direction Study*). These five articles were later published together in 1935 with the title of *Fūikō shiryō zōho* (*Data for the Study of Wind Direction*; Yanagita 1935), which attracted the attention of many folklorists and meteorologists (see Table 1).

For example, historical meteorology reveals important information about Japanese nautical culture in relation to winds and weather conditions. Kitami (1972; Yoshino 1979, p. 166) researched historical navigation and wind seasons in Ryūkyū and Okinawa. His studies reveal, for example, folk classifications of local winds used by local fishermen in Ryūkyū: *nishi kaze*, a northern wind blows on March 21 and on April 5, the easterly wind called *kuchi kaze* on June 21, or during May 6 or 21 and June 6 *hēno kaze*, a southerly wind, blows. According to modern climatology and meteorology, these particular days are called 'singularities' (Yoshino 1979, p. 166) when specific winds blow. The way the wind rose also determined different typologies of navigation in Kyūshu, which were affected strongly by monsoons (Kitami 1972). Among many other Japanese meteorologists, Takeshi Sekiguchi (2000) paid special attention to Yanagita's

Table 1 Some examples of local wind names collected by Kunio Yanagita in *Fūikō shiryō* (1935).

Wind name	Direction	Local place
Yamaji	west	Tadaki, Tokuda-mura
Yamaji	eastsouth	Hokujo, Taga-mura
Yamase	northeast	Hakodate
Yamaze	east	Aomori-ken and Akita-shi
Yamase	northeast	Minamiakita-gun
Yamaji	north	Kosagawa, Yuri-gun and Nishitagawa-gun
Yamaji	southwest	Sakata Port
Yamase	northeast	Tobishima
Yamase	east	Sadogashima Island
Yamase	southeast	Kanazawa-shi
Yamase	northeast	Matsutou
Yamaze	south	East part of Tottori-ken and Izumo, Shimane-ken
Yamaze	south	Iki
Yamase	east	Hokkaidō
Yamase	southwest	Shonai and Houmi-gun, Yamagata-ken
Fujikata, Fujiminami	westsouth	Tōkyō and surroundings
Fujinarai	westsouth	Shimousakatori-gun, Chiba-ken
Fujioroshi	northeast	Mitsuke, Toumi and Hamamatsu
Yamaji, Yamaze	southeast	Iyo
Yamaji	southeast	Kijima

Fūikō Shiryō. In 1980, he sent a questionnaire to survey Japanese fishing cooperatives, collecting 2036 wind names (Sekiguchi 2000, p. 5), and published the collected results in a dictionary entitled *Kaze no jiten* (*Dictionary of Winds*; 1985). Sekiguchi reported 2145 wind names, which he divided into three categories (Sekiguchi 2000, pp. 12–13): wind names used by shipping traders, coastal fishermen, and wind names used in local areas (Sekiguchi 2000, pp. 13–14). Schematically, Sekiguchi has proposed the following wind classification, including wind names derived from Japanese literature (Sekiguchi 2000, p. 14):

(1) Traders' winds

Many wind names for traders were affected by dialects in Kyōto and Ōsaka. Many of them were favourable winds mainly used in west Japan and on the Sea of Japan side of the country. The most frequently used pairs of wind name were *kamikaze* and *shimokaze*, *takaikaze* and *hikuikaze*, *kudari* and *nobori*. *Ai*, *ae*, and *ayunokaze* were often used instead of *nobori*.

(2) Coastal fishermen's winds
   1. Western Japan
      (a) *Anaji*: northwest winter wind

(b) *Maji, hae*: south winter wind
   (c) *Yamaji*: stormy wind
 2. Japan seaside
   (a) *Tamakaze, tabakaze*: northwest winter wind
   (b) *Kudari*: south summer wind
 3. Eastern Japan – Pacific Ocean side
   (a) *Narai, saga, shimosa, bettō, nishi*: winter winds
   (b) *Minami*: south summer wind
   (c) *Inasa*: stormy wind
(3) Winds in limited local areas

These names were used only at the coastal area or in a bay. The names can be divided into three groups:

   (a) Used only in west Japan: *sagari, tosa, youzu, waita*
   (b) Used only on the Sea of Japan side: *wakasa, yamase*
   (c) Used only on the Pacific Ocean side in east Japan: *akanbonarai, saga, shimosa, nakanishi*.
(4) Winds throughout Japan blowing between a mountain and the sea

These names were not used by traders.

   (a) Wind from the sea: *Okikaze, urakaze*
   (b) Wind from the land and mountain: *jikaze, dashi, yamase, arashi*.

(5) Winds in Japanese literature

Wind names used in Japanese literature such as *haiku* and novels:

   (a) *Kaiyose*
   (b) *Kōyama*
   (c) *Tōjinbō*
   (d) *Takanishi*
   (e) *Aokita*

(6) Winds on lakes

Wind names at Lake Biwa and some lower part of the Tone River such as Kasumigaura and Kitaura:

   (a) *Hira*
   (b) *Ibuki*
   (c) *Tsukubaoroshi*

Using a different approach, folklorist Fumitaka Nomura (1995; see Table 2) proposed a system of classification based on geographic regions, prefectures, cities and fishing villages that is less rich and detailed than Sekiguchi's dictionary

Table 2 Classification of local winds (Nomura 1995, p. 128; see also Sekiguchi 2000, Handō and Arakawa 2001, Nakayama 2009).

Geographic area	\multicolumn{9}{c}{Wind direction / Wind names}								
	N	NE	E	SE	S	SW	W	NW
North Ise Bay	*Kita*	*Betō*	*Kochi*	*Inasa*	*Maze*	*Yamaze*	*Manishi*	*Nakanishi*
Tsu-shi	*Kita*	*Kitagochi*	*Kochi*	*Minami-gochi*	*Maze*	*Yamaze*	*Manishi*	*Nakanishi*
Ohama-chō, Toba-shi	*Kitappo*	*Betō*	*Kochi, Mago-Chi*	*Inasa*	*Maze*	*Nishi-Yamaze*	*Nishi, Manishi*	*Nakanishi*
Kamishima-chō, Toba-shi	*Kitappo*	*Narai*	*Kochi*	*Inasa*	*Maze*	*Hikata*	*Nishi*	*Nakanishi*
Sugashima-chō, Toba-shi	*Kita*	*Higashikaze, Hagachi (Typhoon)*	*Kochi*		*Maze*	*Manishi*	*Nishi*	*Nakanishi*
Sankasho, Isobe-chō, Shima-gun	*Kitappo*	*Betō*	*Kochi*	*Inasa*	*Maze*	*Hikatamaze*	*Dashi*	*Hikata*
Anori, Ago-chō, Shima-gun	*Kitappo*	*Narai*	*Kochi*	*Inasa*	*Maze*	*Hikata, Yamaze*	*Manishi*	*Nakanishi*
Gokasho, Nansei-chō, Watarai-gun	*Kitappo*	*Makata, Narai*	*Kochi*	*Inasa*	*Maze*	*Yamaze, Tosa*	*Nishi, Manishi*	*Nishikaze, Anaze, Nakanishi*
Nieura, Nanto-chō, Watarai-gun	*Kitappo*	*Kochi*	*Higashi*	*Inasa*	*Maze*	*Jimaze*	*Nishi*	*Nakanishi*
Kiinagashima-chō, Kitamuro-gun	*Kita*	*Kitagochi (Narai)*	*Kochi*	*Inasa*	*Maze*	*Nishimaze, Waita*	*Manishi*	*Serai, Nakanishi*
Nishiki, Kisei-chō, Kitamuro-gun	*Kitappo*	*Youzu*	*Kochi*	*Inasa*	*Maze*	*Narai*	*Manishi*	*Nakanishi*
Kuki-chō, Owase-shi	*Narai*	*Kitakochi*	*Kochi*	*Inasa*	*Maze*	*Jimaze*	*Nishi*	*Nakanishi*
Kajiga-chō, Owase-shi	*Kitappo*	*Kitagochi*	*Kochi*	*Inasa*	*Maze*	*Hae, Maze*	*Nishi*	*Nakanishi*
Utome-mura, Minamimuro-gun	*Makita*	*Kitagochi*	*Kochi*	*Inasa, Yamaze*	*Maze*	*Yamaze*	*Manishi*	*Nakanishi*
Morozaki, Aichi-ken	*Kitappo*	*Betō*	*Kochi*	*Inasa*	*Maze*	*Yamaze*	*Sumanishi*	*Nakanishi*
Higashihazu, Aichi-ken	*Kitappo*	*Betou, Naraigochi*	*Kochi*	*Inasagochi*	*Maze*	*Yamaze*	*Sumanishi*	*Nakanishi*
Tosa, Kōchi-ken	*Kita, Yamagita*	*Kamige*	*Kochi*	*Jimaji, Inasa, Inasakaze Tamakaze*	*Maji, Minamiarase, Hibarigochi*	*Maji, Nishmaze, Sanishi, Minami*	*Nishi*	*Kitagochi, Ibuki, Yamagita, Ohgita*
Shimokita-gun, Aomori-ken	*Ai, Kita*	*Shimokaze Yamase, Ainokaze*	*Yamase*	*Minami-Yamase*	*Minami, Kudari*	*Hikata, Shikata*	*Nishi, Nishikaze*	*Tamakaze*
Noto Peninsula, Ishikawa-ken	*Tabagachi*	*Aitabagachi, Nishi-Tabakatsu, Saraidashi*	*Ai, Maai*	*Yasuai, Zenkouji-Mon Shimo-Dashi*	*Kudari, Makudari*	*Sikata, Nishi-Shikata*	*Nishikaze, Shikata, Shitaki*	*Takakaze, Nishishikata, Uranishi*
Fukui-ken	*Ai*	*Jiai, Shimoarashi, Shimo-Isomon*	*Arashi, Isomon*	*Jikudari, Kami-Arashi, Kami-Isomon*	*Kudari*	*Taka-Kudari, Kami-Nishi*	*Nishi*	*Takaai, Shimonishi, Shimoshiraba*
Uchiura, Osaki-chō, Toyota-gun, Hiroshima-ken	*Kita*	*Kitagochi*	*Kochi*	*Yamaji-Gochi*	*Yamaji*	*Takanishi*	*Nishi*	*Anaji*
Uchimado-chō, Okayama-ken	*Kita*	*Kitagochi, Sagegochi*	*Kochi*	*Yamaji*	*Maji*		*Nishi*	*Anaji*
Genkai, Fukuoka-ken	*Kita*	*Kitagochi*	*Kochi*	*Jikaze*	*Hae*	*Sagari-Nishi*	*Nishi*	*Negita, Anaze*
Amakusa, Kumamoto-ken	*Kita*	*Kitagochi*	*Kochi*	*Kochihae*	*Hae*	*Okibae*	*Nishi*	*Anaze*

but gives a more comparative perspective on fishermen's wind taxonomies. Independent of these different levels of wind classification, the extraordinary number of meteorological words used by Japanese fishermen defines a sort of 'textual landscape': the dynamic relationship and interdependencies between fishing communities, local economies and the environment are a process in which the sensory qualities of the landscape interact with classification practices, which orient fishermen's strategies in making decisions that involve potential meteorological risks. As we will see in the next section, recognition and classification of winds play a key role in the strategies of Kuzaki-chō fishermen (Ise Bay) based on two interdependent factors. First, the wind regime in Kuzaki-chō is a complex meteorological phenomenon, because the effects of baric conditions associated with orography, affect the productivity of local fisheries. Second, the relationship between local climate variability and the resulting adaptations of coastal fisheries is essential for Kuzaki-chō fishermen to understand strategies that are based on the ability to assess a number of climate-environmental factors that influence the social behaviour of fished species, subject to fluctuations caused by environmental factors (sea temperature, ocean currents) and atmospheric phenomena (seasonal winds and strong perturbations). In this context, fishermen create a rich cultural tapestry of their local climate and maritime environment, particularly through their recognition of the values they attach to their everyday places, concomitant sense of place, landscapes and personal memories. As we will see, these factors are strategically important to understand the distinctiveness of fishermen's experiences inextricably interwoven with meanings associated with places, landscapes and the cultural forms in which fishermen's memories are inscribed.

Sedimented experiences

In Kuzaki-chō, a small coastal community of Shima Peninsula located to the south of Ise Bay, the opportunity to haul in a good catch pushes small boats to work offshore, where the Kuroshio ocean current ('black current', due to the intense blue of its waters) makes the coastal regions well stocked with fish. Ise Bay is a geographic area particularly exposed to atmospheric phenomena of great intensity (typhoons, winds and potentially meteorological hazards), subject to a high risk of disaster for fishermen. Among various activities carried out by local fishing cooperatives, the dissemination of weather forecasts provided by the Coast Guard is a task performed by the *kumiaichō* (director of the fishing cooperative). However, in the case of the community of Kuzaki-chō, the diffusion of local weather forecasts is often a cause of friction between members of the cooperative and the *kumiaichō*. Dolores Martinez (2004, 2008), who conducted extensive research on the community of Kuzaki-chō in the early 1980s, gives an interesting account of the dynamics that triggered conflicts between fishermen and local institutions revolving around a weather report, because 'science was not considered totally reliable in predicting what might happen in nature' (Martinez 2008, p. 189) or because 'the cooperative head hesitated because of weather reports that predicted a rapid change, then those afternoons were spent in increasingly acrimonious discussions' (Martinez 2008, p. 189).

According to Martinez (2008), Kuzaki-chō fishermen's cultural responses to the 'contested' information provided by the coastguard weather service were the study of clouds and tides, type of waves, the phase of the moon, asking women with some sort of sense about weather forecasting or consulting experienced elders 'to see if on other days in other years such weather had ever turned' (Martinez 2008, p. 189). Although Martinez does not focus on the taxonomy of local weather phenomena, instead focusing her attention on the relationship between the religious system and the local genderized economy (Martinez 2004), these quotes stir interest because they reflect how Kuzaki-chō fishermen's personal memories, skills and ecological knowledge try to answer the most pressing question (Martinez 2008, p. 189):

> It was not that the fishermen did not believe that the weather at sea could change rapidly – they were acutely aware of the fact that men died at sea even in what seemed the calmest of conditions – but the question would be whether the timescale of the weather report was seen as accurate: would the change in weather happen later than predicted, giving enough time to come back with fishing done? Would the change be so drastic? Would the storm even reach the coasts?

Trying to contribute to broaden the horizons of Martinez's ethnography, the analysis of the classification of winds elaborated by Kuzaki-chō fishermen is an example of the acceptance and coexistence with natural risks, which suggests an almost symbiotic relationship between fishermen and meteorological risks. The local economy is based primarily on fishing *awabi* (*Haliotis sorensen*, abalone) and *ise ebi* (*Panulirus japonicus*, lobster). During May, October and December, *awabi* is caught by *ama*, female divers who are distinguished into two categories according to the method of fishing: *funado* (boat-based) and *kachido* (walking diver). *Funado* uses a boat with her husband: she dives into the ocean while her husband drives the boat; *kachido* instead immerses herself into the sea, starting from the beach (Martinez 2004). *Ise ebi* fishing requires instead the use of *sashi ami* (gill-net) and most of the boats operate within a kilometre from the coast. These activities have a strong seasonality: *ise ebi* fishing starts in the second half of November and continues until the end of April, although fishermen are allowed to fish only forty days per season, according to the regulations. The period of fishing for octopus is instead from June to September, during the period in which they leave the ocean to 'fall' into Ise Bay (the phenomenon of migration is locally called *nobori dako*, meaning 'octopus rising'). A fishing technique widely practised for the capture of *ise ebi*, is so-called *yama ate* (allocate the mountain), a cognitive grid that consists of a set of lines of position to define the territories of coastal fisheries and to determine the fishing licences. Kuzaki-chō fishermen use the expression *yama atewo miru* (watch *yama ate*) to refer to this guidance system to locate the exact position of the rocks where *ise ebi* and *awabi* take refuge. In fishing strategies, this technique plays a very important role in local fisheries, because it is a traditional technique of orientation (Igarashi 1974, Kawahara *et al.* 2005) that is combined with knowledge about the landscape and the dynamics of local winds.

Kuzaki-chō fishermen have their own expressions for wind rose: *kitappo* (north), *bettō* also called *kitagochi* (north-east), *kochi* and *hongochi* (east),[8] *inasa* (south-east), *maze* (south), *hikata* (south-west), *nishi* (west) and *hokusei* or *oroshi* (north-west) (Nomura 1995, Sekiguchi 2000, Nakayama 2009). The northern wind from Honshu is called *kitappo*, which frequently brings rain and strong disturbances for the maritime species and is the cause of maritime disasters. The most dangerous wind is *bettō* or *kitagochi*, a north-east wind that heralds the arrival of a typhoon. Generally, fishermen know that when a typhoon is coming from the south approaching Ise Bay *bettō* begins to blow and then it gradually changes into *kitappo*.[9] Depending on the season, *inasa* and *kochi* may herald bad weather; *hongochi* is another type of *kochi*, which blows when low pressure comes along the coast of the Pacific Ocean between March and April. According to local fishermen, if a warm south wind changes into *inasa*, it means that the weather will worsen and they do not go out to sea. The south wind is called instead *maze* (Sekiguchi 2000, p. 829) and blows in the spring and summer, announcing the arrival of summer. The hot wind that blows from west is called *hikata* and marks the beginning of spring. Generally, after having blown *hikata*, the temperature starts to rise, followed by light rain. The west winter wind is simply called *nishi* (west) and it is a reigning wind, and finally *oroshi* is a wind that blows from mount Asakuma (north of Kuzaki-chō) and it is one of the prevailing winter winds of Ise Bay (Owada and Ishikawa 1994, Nakayama 2009).

Among the winds known by fishermen, *kochi* is the most dangerous wind. There is a proverb respected by local fishermen: *aki no kochiha tomoami o kitte nigero demo* (if you feel *kochi* blows in autumn while you're off, you have to go back even if you have to cut the anchor rope). During autumn, a seasonal wind like *kochi* can blow on coastal waters at a speed that varies between 13 and 18 knots, generating waves of over two metres. These 'white sea waves', coming from the east, are the main threat for fishermen, given that a small boat can easily tip over if hit by one of these waves. The meaning of this proverb lies in knowing how to interpret the first signs of bad weather, feeling the rapid change of waves and wind. However, *kochi* is also a wind that may have a positive influence on determining fisheries' local productivity: when *kochi* starts to blow and the sea becomes rough, the fishermen go out to sea, when the weather conditions still allow it, to place *sashi ami* off the coast. The explanation provided by fishermen was very simple: when the sea is rough it creates a current on the seabed that 'pushes' lobsters offshore. Knowing how to position fishing nets in the area where lobsters are moving, using the technique of *yama ate*, in many cases guarantees a great catch. Unlike *kochi*, the west wind (*nishi*) and the northwest wind (*oroshi*), generated by the winter monsoon, are the strongest winds in Ise Bay and generally dominate from November to April (Owada and Ishikawa 1994, Nakayama 2009). These winds are dangerous for local fishermen because the western part of Kuzaki-chō is protected by a hilly area, which extends to the town of Ōsatsu (south of Kuzaki-chō). Although these winds are not dangerous thanks to the hills that reduce their intensity, the cold airflow of *oroshi* affects *ise ebi* fishery. Water temperature is a very important factor because it directly influences the social behaviour of the *ise ebi*: this species becomes sedentary when water gets cold, while an increase in temperature causes migratory movements. For this reason, one of the most favourable winds for fishing is *maze*, because it blows on hot days, raising the water temperature.[10]

Another important aspect of the cultural dynamics of local weather is the relationship between *ama* and seasonal winds (Nomura 1995). *Awabi* fishing, like any underwater activity, requires visibility of the seabed, and *ama* avoid fishing when *kochi* is blowing, because during atmospheric disturbances the sand raised by marine currents hinders the *awabi*. *Ama* generally describe this phenomenon with a saying: *sunaga soko kara kuru fuite* (sand blows from the bottom of the sea), an expression that implies almost an alternation in fishing practices, in which winds influence all aspects of working life. Similar to the meteorological dynamics affecting *ise ebi* fishery is *namako* (sea cucumber) fishing, in which a cold west wind plays a strategic role. *Namako* come out from a reef when *nishi* pushes cold water from Ise Bay to the Ocean and the water temperature drops (Nakayama 2009). When a clear tide runs out from Ise Bay after the *nishi* wind stops blowing, seawater becomes clear and *ama* can fish. This symbiotic relationship between women divers and local winds is found also in Kamishima-chō, a small island located off the coast of Ise Bay, where local *ama* can predict wind dynamics just by observing seabed movement even before the wind blows.[11]

The complexity with which local fishermen and *ama* describe the multiple views of the maritime environment or construct meaningful relationships with their surroundings and wind regime, are critical elements of the negotiated past, too. Through narratives and memories of generations of fishermen, winds interact constantly with the past and present life of fishermen who define their 'own weather', often in contestation with scientific weather prediction. Winds become thus part of fishermen's cultural horizon, acting as protagonists of nautical stories, proverbs and personal memories. As will be seen, rough winds or gentle breezes that blow in Ise Bay, constitute a sort of 'invisible landscape' linguistically defined (as seen in the previous section) and conceived as a web of interactions between knowledge, perceptions, memories and practices.

Invisible landscapes

As seen in the previous section, Japanese fishermen have different descriptions of the interactions and effects of meteorological forces operating in the local ecosystem, and seasonal winds assume a significant role in the predictions of seasonal climatic characteristics that influence the local economies. As a container of physical and cognitive entities, the landscape is embedded in a network of eco-semiotic interactions (Farina 2010). According to Niamh Moore and Yvonne Whealm (2007, p. 4), landscapes 'exist reflexively in our cognitive as well as our corporeal experiences of the material world, shaping and being shaped by our simultaneously multiple identities as humans. [...] Its connection with the realms of the cognitive and mnemonic, and so with the general issue of consciousness (including "non-consciousness", in the sense of Bourdieu's "habitus"), is therefore inalienable'. In such terms, landscapes, in an anthropological sense, are those portions of space linked to the 'identity of space', inextricably inter-connected with the production of meanings and identity construction through symbols and cultural images associated with landscape (Relph 1976). 'Space' becomes a 'place' (Feld and Basso 1996) only through narrative and codes of perception, 'supplied by the horizons and depth of existence' (Casey 1996, p. 18) The ethnographic case of Kuzaki-chō fishermen reveals how wind connects fishermen with the environment, and how perception of winds is embodied in cultural practices and linguistic expressions, such as wind classifications and proverbs.

In the Japanese language, the word for wind (*kaze*; *fū* in compound words) reveals a semantic complexity in terms of the definition of the landscape: *fūkei* or *fūō* (scenery, landscape), *fūgetsu* (beauties of nature), *fūbutsu* (natural features, scenery), *fūun* (winds and clouds), *fūu* (winds and rain), *fūchi* (scenic zone, a landscape area), *fūha* (winds and waves, rough sea), or *fūdo* (natural features, climate or spiritual features). Vernacular words are closely associated with the perception of landscape: for example, the fishermen of Anori, a small community located in Motoya Bay, use the word *hikata* to indicate a southwest wind that blows in spring and summer. *Hikata* is considered a 'broom wind' by local fishermen, because when it blows, the colour of the sea becomes dark, driving away fish stocks off the coast until they are 'cleared away' (Nomura 1995). Arai-chō fishermen (Atami-shi, Izu peninsula) call *nishi* (west) a winter spring wind that blows from the west for more than a week, causing a lowering of the temperature, which prevents fishing. *Yukinarai* (Hihashizu-chō, Izu peninsula) is a strong and dangerous north-west wind that blows in February with snowy rain causing bad visibility at sea (Nomura 1995). Fishermen describe winds with adjectives related to universal categories of fishing culture: scary, calm, gentle, dangerous, harmful, good, bad, strong, weak, violent, or using sensory adjectives (warm, chilly, cold), colours (black, white), or vernacular terms such as *oya no kaze* (parent wind) and *ko kaze* (child wind) to indicate specific interrelated local winds that blow from the land to the sea. Winds are also described as related to other atmospheric phenomena, such as rain, snow or typhoon, human health (headache), or directly related to the behaviour of the target species: *tai* (sea bream), *namako* (sea cucumber), *katsuo* (bonito), *warasa* (yellowtail), and so on.

Winds are undoubtedly the protagonists of fishermen's stories of shipwrecks and maritime disasters. In this context, proverbs generally imply a summary of the wisdom of collective experience, usually determined by factors such as memory, and used by members of a cultural group to communicate interpretations of interactional situations (Hasan-Roken 1992, p. 129). In Japan, a number of proverbs about winds exist and, in many cases, they are not relegated to the immovable Japanese folk literary archives, but still have an active role among fishing communities. As seen in the previous paragraph, Kuzaki-chō fishermen's proverb becomes implicitly a weather rule that reveals how a specific wind plays a strategic role in local fish productivity and, at the same time, it highlights a meteorological risk. Another example, in which I could verify the roles of proverbs as 'agents of memory' among fishing communities where I did my fieldwork, are two well-known proverbs in the area of Kumanonada Sea: 'west wind after *yamaze* is scary' and 'west wind after *yamaze* is dangerous as a dog that eats humans'. These lapidary sentences generally show that the west wind in Kumanonada Sea is another wind that has played an import role in the past and present experiences of local fishermen.

According to the historical archives of Kamishima-chō, the local fishing community suffered three maritime accidents: 13 fishermen died at sea as a result of a west wind on 13 April 1750, other 53 on 4 March 1763 and 121 men died at sea on 25 March 1800, killing almost all the men of working age on this island, forcing the community to adopt boys and young men from Owari-chō, Tsu-shi, Mikawa-chō and Atsuta-ku to keep their family lineage. According to Nomura (1995, p. 135) this proverb explains succinctly those tragic episodes: local fishermen's interpretations explained that all accidents were caused by a spring gust in March or April (according to the traditional lunar calendar), or May (according to the solar calendar) when *maze* (south wind) and *yamaze* (southwest wind) were blowing on the days of the accident and were suddenly replaced by a strong west wind that pushed the fishing boats off to Enshu.

During my conversations with Kamishima-chō fishermen, winds were really an important topic and 'scary winds' occupied a central role in the narrated events. Sometimes winds were indirectly reconnected to other individual and collective experiences such as the water resources strategies adopted on the island. In Japan, water resources are not evenly distributed throughout the archipelago, because of the different hydrogeological characteristics of the islands and their geographical location. Indeed, until 1980, Kamishima-chō community suffered the same situation of hydrological scarcity as many other remote islands (*ritō*) before the interventions made by the Japanese Government. In an attempt to achieve a balance of self-management and self-sufficiency, the villagers carried out a series of initiatives to ensure efficient use of local water resources. In some cases, especially in summer, fishermen had to ship to Toba-shi in order to bring back drinking water, and winds could be a serious problem for the stability of the boat.

And finally, seasonal winds are connected to Kamishima-chō's historical settlement, becoming part of the fishermen's urban landscape. The relationship between the circulation of the regimes of local winds and rural settlement shows patterns of understanding of the conditions of local ventilation, which is essential as part of strategies to enhance the efficiency of rural settlements. The island is located in very turbulent waters, it is bordered by the sea of Enshu in the east and the Sea of Kumano in the west, a difficult area to navigate, while on the northern side it faces the Irago Canal, an extremely dangerous current sea, due to its proximity to the Pacific Ocean. Featuring as a compact, rounded island, Kamishima-chō is presented as mainly mountainous, particularly exposed to atmospheric phenomena of great intensity. For this reason the village was built in the northern part of the island, because the mountains protect it from strong gusts of winds and typhoons. The interdependence of land and community has resulted in a rural structure characterized by a concentrated agglomeration located in a very narrow area, which occupies completely the northern side of the island, linking the local beach longitudinally with the mouth of the Kamishima-chō's harbour. The planimetric scheme of the rural settlement is based on a set of streets, lined by a continuous system of houses, which converge at the main street of the village. There are streets in which the winter wind blows violently: *hanaka tōge* (red nose mountain pass, to indicate the nasal congestion), for example, is a slope that connects *gori no hama* (old village beach), a place inhabited in the past but then abandoned due to exposure to typhoon winds. Near *gori no hama* there is a place called *kaze no kami* (wind god), proving the fact that the whole south area of the island is particularly exposed to strong wind gusts.

This verbal-folkloristic creativity of place naming is structured around the space-time references that strengthen personal and collective memories of this fishing community. Based on the ethnographic descriptions given above, it could therefore be argued that these places, strictly connected to seasonal winds, open up a whole scenario of memories with a strong emotional aura (community water management) or their association with images of the historical past of the local surroundings (nautical stories), landscape perception (proverbs) or the historical settlement of the community.

Conclusions

Wind experience in Japanese coastal fisheries derives from centuries of 'situated environmental practices' (Ingold 2003, p. 227) becoming a structural factor of perception of landscape for two reasons. As the meaning imputed by local people to their physical surroundings, wind perception assumes a structural value, because fishermen establish a whole series of cultural practices, which generate an anthropized landscape, as a function of how they perceive their environment. Secondly, as we have seen, winds are directly connected to processes such as fishermen's sense of belonging to a specific place and geographical areas. According to this perspective, winds are not simply part of a 'mindscape' (Zerubavel 2009), in which fishermen's memories of 'sedimented experiences' are a cultural substratum – to be reminded of Ingold's definition of MTK (traditional knowledge in modernist conception, see Ingold 2000, p. 307) – but are complementary components of an embodied landscape, in which memory actively operates to define fishermen's past and present experiences.

As we have seen, landscape and all its components (winds, sea waves, sea bottom, beaches, coasts, boats, fish, etc.) should therefore not be understood as a physical container in which to place an objectified cultural heritage, but as a space in continuous construction and an environmental arena for negotiations and contestations between fishermen's knowledge, memories and other institutional knowledge. Drawing on this perspective, this article has also sought to contribute to the effort to redefine the interpretive approaches of Japanese folklore studies. The theme of 'contested memory' on an apparently marginal topic such as wind may make us reflect on how to recontextualize the role of memory not as a repository of a vanishing heritage, as Japanese folklore studies suggest, but as an interpretative process. The ethnographic cases, reconnecting to contributions made by this academic discipline, have attempted to demonstrate how memory is shaped in order to replace itself in this dialectical relationship between landscape and local fishermen: through language (the classification of the winds, proverbs, dialect terms, experiences narrated), space (in which the production of memory binds individuals in a sphere of shared meanings) and time (in which memory acts as the direct testimony of individual and collective spheres of work experience). In this context, wind assumes significance in the discursive practices of active memory, which ultimately defines a 'geographical biography' among Japanese coastal fishermen.

Disclosure statement

No potential conflict of interest was reported by the author.

Notes

1. In this article I propose an interpretative model built around the anthropological idea that landscape represents the product of a cultural process, in which the symbolic aspects are closely linked to economic, social and economic ones. The landscape is therefore a culturally constructed, perceptual process of representation, organization and classification of the space, a way of ordering experience, a complex process that involves cultural expectations and the potential of a given community (Hirsch and O'Hanlon 1995, pp. 1–30).
2. The term *minzokugaku* conventionally is translated as 'folklore studies' or 'ethnology', even if they differ graphically. In this article I use the translation 'folklore studies' as the bibliographic material I used refers mainly to this type of discipline.
3. Fieldwork note (2008).

4. The cultural phenomenology has contributed decisively to introduce the paradigm of incorporation into anthropology. According to Csordas, the work of Merleau-Ponty (1945), helps anthropology to break away from a notion of the body as the site for the recognition of symbolic meanings to adopt the paradigm of incorporation (Csordas 1994), offering a new perspective on aspects of culture that have been faced with a semiotic approach.
5. Originally developed by Satoru Yasumuro (2008), 'nariwai complex' refers to various productive skills that are combined in order to create a supply system for a person or a household (Nomoto 2008).
6. Himawari or Geostationary Meteorological Satellites (GMS) was a series of Japanese weather satellites operated by the Japan Meteorological Agency (JMA). When Nomura published his book, the fifth and final Himawari satellite was launched 18 March 1995 from Tanegashima.
7. In winter, the anticyclone developed by the cold Asiatic continent develops a cold, dry polar-continental air-stream centrifugally oceanward. This is the winter monsoon of China and Japan, which is replaced in summer by the weaker and more intermittent southeast summer monsoon, originating from the warmer parts of Pacific Ocean and converging upon eastern Asia.
8. According to Sekiguchi (2000, p. 414), *kochi* is also called *ōgochi*.
9. Fieldwork note (2009).
10. This wind is also known by Japanese fishermen under the name of *abura kaze* or *abura maji* (wind oil) because it is quiet, like shed oil (Handō and Arakawa 2001, p. 18).
11. Fieldwork note (2008); see also Nomura (1995) and Nakayama (2009).

References

Acheson, J., 1981. Anthropology of fishing. *Annual Review of Anthropology*, 10, 275–316.
Aono, T., 1938. Izuhantō ni okeru kazemachikō (Waiting wind ports of the Izu Peninsula). *Chiri*, 1 (2), 234–249.
Bachelard, G., 1964. *The poetics of space*. Boston: Beacon Press.
Berkes, F., 1999. *Sacred ecology: traditional ecological knowledge and resource management*. Philadelphia: Taylor and Francis.
Berkes, F. and Folke C., eds. 1998. *Linking social and ecological systems: management practices and social mechanisms for building resilience*. Cambridge: Cambridge University Press.
Bourdieu, P., 1990. *The logic of practice*. Stanford: Stanford University Press.
Casey, S.E., 1996. How to get from space to place in a fairly short stretch of time: phenomenological prolegomena. *In*: S. Feld and K.H. Basso, eds. *Senses of place*. Santa Fe: School of American Research Press, 13–52.
Csordas, J.T., 1994. *Embodiment and experience: the existential ground of culture and self*. Cambridge: Cambridge University Press.
Ellen, R. and Harris, H., 2000. Introduction. *In:* R. Ellen, P. Parker and A. Bicker, eds. *Indigenous environmental knowledge and its transformations*. Amsterdam: Harwood Academic Publishers.
Farina, A. 2010. *Ecology, Cognition and Landscape, Linking Natural and Social Systems*. Dordrecht, Heidelberg, London, and New York: Springer.
Feld, S. and Basso, K.H. 1996. Introduction. *In:* S. Feld and K.H. Basso, eds. *Senses of place*. Santa Fe: School of American Research Press, 3–12.
Gray, J. 2000. *At home in the hills: sense of place in the Scottish Borders*. Oxford: Berghahn.
Handō, K. and Hiroshi, A., 2001. *Kaze no namae Kaze no shiki* (Name of the winds – Winds of four seasons). Tokyo: Heibonsha.
Hasan, R., 1992. Proverb. *In:* R. Bauman, ed. *Folklore, cultural performances and popular entertainments: a communications-centered handbook*. New York: Oxford University Press, 128–133.

Hassan, F., 2000. Environmental perception and human responses in history and prehistory. *In:* R. J. McIntosh, J.A. Tainter and S. Keech McIntosh, eds. *The way the wind blows: climate, history and human action.* New York: Columbia University Press, 121–140.

Hirsch, E. and O'Hanlon, M., 1995. Introduction. Between place and space. *In:* E. Hirsch and M. O'Hanlon, eds. *The anthropology of landscape: perspectives on place and space.* Oxford: Clarendon Press, 1–30.

Hsu, E. and Low, C., 2008. Introduction. *In:* E. Hsu and C. Low, eds. *Wind, life, health: anthropological and historical perspectives.* Oxford: Blackwell Publishing.

Igarashi, T., 1974. A traditional technique of fishermen for locating fishing spots: a case study in the Tokara islands. *Journal of Human Ergology,* 3 (1), 3–28.

Ingold, T., 2000. *The perception of the environment: essays on livelihood, dwelling and skill.* London: Routledge.

Ingold, T., 2003. Two reflections on ecological knowledge. *In:* G. Sanga and G. Ortalli, eds. *Nature knowledge: ethnoscience, cognition, and utility.* New York: Berghahn Books.

Ivy, M., 1995. *Discourses of the Vanishing: modernity, phantasm.* Japan, London: The University of Chicago Press.

Kalland, A., 1994. Indigenous knowledge: prospects and limitations. *In:* R. Ellen, P. Parkes Peter and A. Bicker, eds. *Indigenous environmental knowledge and its transformations: critical anthropological perspectives.* London: Harwood.

Kawahara, N., Saitō, K., *et al.,* 2005. 'GPS o mochiita yama ate wo meguru chirigaku kenkyū no hōhō-teki shiron' (Methodological essay on geography research over the Yama ate using GPS). *Ritsumeikan chirigaku,* 17, 79–86.

Kitami, T., 1972. *Kōwan sōron' (A study of the harbors), Kōwan Kenkyū Shirizu.* Tokyo: Naruyamadō shoten.

Martinez, D., 2004. *Identity and ritual in a Japanese diving village: the making and becoming of person and place.* Honolulu: University of Hawai'i Press.

Martinez, D., 2008. On the "nature" of Japanese culture, or, is there a Japanese sense of nature? *In:* J. Robertson, ed. *A companion to the anthropology of Japan.* Oxford: Blackwell Publishing.

Merleau-Ponty, M., 1945. *Phénoménologie de la Perception.* Paris: Gallimard.

Moore, N. and Yvonne, W., eds. 2007. *Heritage, memory and the politics of identity: new perspectives on the cultural landscape.* Chippenham: Ashgate.

Mori, A., 2014. Japan. *In:* R.F. Bendix and G. Hasan-Rokem, eds. *A companion to folklore.* Oxford: Wiley-Blackwell.

Nadasdy, P., 1997. The politics of TEK: power and the "integration" of knowledge. *Arctic Anthropology,* 36 (1–2), 1–1.

Nakayama, M., 2009. *Kaze to kankyō no minzoku* (Folklore of environment and wind). Tokyo: Yoshikawa.

Nomoto, K., 1988. Sunaji no nariwai (Subsistence in sandy soil). *In:* Shizuokaken minzoku geinō kenkyūkai, ed., *Umi no minzokushi* (Folklore of the sea). Shizuoka shinbunsha.

Nomoto, K., 2008. Nariwai minzoku kenkyū no yukue (Future of folkloric research on subsistence). *In: Nariwai kara miru nipponshi – atarashī rekishigaku no shatei* (Japanese historical view of subsistence - New range of history). Tokyo: Yoshikawakōbunkan.

Nomura, F., 1995. Kaze no minzoku (Folklore of wind). *In:* A. Mitsuo, K. Kazuhiko, F. Ajio, K. Yōichirō, N. Kan'ichi, eds. *Kankyo no minzoku* (Folklore of environment), vol. 4. Tokyo: Yūzankaku shuppan, 127–144.

Owada, M. and Ishikawa, Y., 1994. The climatic study of local fronts on a microscale in the Ise Bay and its surrounding areas in Central Japan. *In: Japanese progress in climatology.* Tōkyō: Hosei University, 115–117.

Pàllson, G., 1994. Enskilment at Sea. *Man,* 29 (4), 901–927.

Phelan, J., 2007. *Seascapes: tides of thought and being in Western perceptions of the sea.* Goldsmiths Anthropology Research Papers, London: University of London.

Rappaport J.N., 1997. *Transcendent individual: towards a liberal and literary anthropology.* London: Routledge.

Relph, E., 1976. *Place and placelessness.* London: Pion.

Rigney, A., 2005. Plentitude, scarcity and circulation of cultural memory. *Journal of European Studies,* 35 (1), 11–28.

Robertson, J., 1998. *Furusato* Japan: the culture and politics of nostalgia. *International Journal of Politics, Culture, and Society,* 1 (4), 494–518.

Schell, S. and Hiroyuki, H., 2003. 'Guest Editors' Introduction: revitalizing Japanese folklore. *Asian Folklore Studies,* 62 (2), 185–194.

Sekiguchi, T., 2000. *Kaze no jiten* (Dictionary of winds). Tokyo: Hara Shobō.

Shindo M., 1994. *Seto naikai no sakana to kurashi* (Fishing and life at the western area of the Inland Sea), Kanagawa daigaku nihon jomon bunka sosho. vol. 3. Tokyo: Heibonsha.

Shinohara, T., 1995. *Umi to yama no minzoku shizenshi* (Studies of enviromental folklore of sea and mountains). Tokyo: Yoshikawa kōbunkan.

Suga, Y., 2001. 'Shizen o meguru minzoku kenkyū no mittsu no chōryū' (Three trends of folk research concerning nature). *Nihon minzokugaku,* 227, 14–28.

Yanagi, T., 2008. "Sato-Umi" – A new concept for sustainable fisheries. *In:* K. Tsukamoto., T. Kawamura., T. Takeuchi., T. D. Beard, Jr., and M. J. Kaiser., eds. *Fisheries for global welfare and environment, 5th world fisheries congres.* Tokyo: Terrapub, pp. 351–358.

Yanagita, K., 1935. *Fūikō shiryō zōho* (Data for study of direction of winds). Tokyo: Meiseidō.

Yanagita, K., 1963. Opportunities for Folklore research in Japan. *In:* R.M. Dorson, ed. *Studies in Japanese folklore.* Indiana: Indiana University Press.

Yasumuru, S., 2008. Nariwai no minzoku – fukugo nariwairon no kokoromi (Attempts on theory of complex subsistence). *In: Nariwai kara miru nipponshi atarashi rekishigaku no shatei* (Japanese historical view of subsistence – new range of history). Tokyo: Yoshikawakobunkan.

Yoshino, M., 1979. Winter and summer monsoons and the navigation in East Asia in historical age. *GeoJournal,* 3 (2), 161–170.

Whyte, P.K., 2013. On the role of traditional ecological knowledge as a collaborative concept: a philosophical study. *Ecological processes,* 2 (7). Available from http://www.ecologicalprocesses.com/content/2/1/7.

Wilhelm, H.J., 2003. Traditional ecological knowledge in the beliefs of Japanese fishing villages: with special reference to Yoriiso (Miyagi) and the Sanriku Region. *Japanese Religions,* 30 (1&2), 21–53.

Zerubavel, E., 2009. *Social mindscapes: an invitation to cognitive sociology.* Cambridge: Harvard University Press.

Index

abalone 100
Abe, S. 1, 5, 9, 13–14, 27, 32, 39, 54, 57
accidents 2, 4–7, 15–22, 104
accountability 28, 32, 43–4
Acheson, J. 89
air bases 2, 5–6, 10, 13–15, 19, 21
air crashes 15–22
air force 54
aircraft 5–7, 13, 19, 53
Allies 9
American eagle 4–25
Amnesty International (AI) 37
Anderson, B.R. 75
Anori 103
anthropology 56, 87–8, 92, 103
Arai-chō 103
armies 52, 54–5, 60–1
Asakuma, Mt 101
Asia 26, 28, 30–1, 33, 37–8, 42–3, 59, 94
Asia-Pacific War 1–2, 8, 10, 55, 77
Asō, T. 36
assimilation-association model 74, 78
atomic (A) bombs 11, 30, 80

Berkes, F. 90
Biwa, Lake 97
Bourdieu, P. 92, 103
Brazil 52
Buddhism 66–7, 69
Bulian, G. 3, 80, 85–109
bureaucracy 27, 35, 37–41, 44
Buruma, I. 59
Bush, G.W. 35

censorship 56, 76
China 1, 4, 8–9, 27–8, 43–4, 54, 57, 69, 77
Chiran Peace Memorial Museum 54–5, 58, 60
Christianity 66
citizenship 75

climatology 85, 87, 94–5, 99, 103
co-occurence network analysis 68–9
Coast Guard 99–100
coastal fisheries 2–3, 85–109
Code of Crimes against International Law 41
Cold War 4, 31, 33
collective memory 2, 6–12, 15, 21, 29; coastal fisheries 105; Kamikazes 52, 55–6, 58, 61, 74, 79; war crime tribunals 32
colonialism 8
comfort women 1, 8, 26, 54–5
Commission on the Review of Overseas Military Facility Structure of the United States 18
compensation 27–9, 43
Constitution 34
contestation 1–25, 50–84, 86, 100, 106
Cornerstone of Peace 10–12
critical discourse analysis 73
Croatia 52
culture 3, 8, 33, 56–7, 59–60, 66, 75–6, 79, 85–95, 99–100, 102–6

democracy 14, 29
Democratic Party of Japan 14
demographic studies 62–7
denial 51, 54–8
dialectics 89, 106
dialects 95–6, 106
Diet 26–7, 35–9, 41
diplomacy 1, 43
discourse 51, 54, 56–8, 62, 64; coastal fisheries 88, 91–4, 106; dominant 2–3, 29, 32, 52, 60, 86; Kamikazes 67, 72–4, 76, 78–80
Discourse Historical Approach within Critical Discourse Analysis (DHA-CDA) 72–3
Does-Ishikawa, L. van der 2, 50–84
dominant discourse 2–3, 29, 32, 52, 60, 86
Dower, J. 54

INDEX

East Asia 9, 54
ecology 3, 85–7, 89–94, 100
economics 58, 75, 86–8, 99–100, 103
Edo Period 95
education 6, 8, 29, 31, 51–2, 56, 61–2, 64, 69–73, 75–7, 79
elites 29, 63
embodiment 28, 37–8, 40, 43, 87–8, 91, 103, 106
emotion 3, 51, 56–60, 69–74, 76, 79, 105
Enshu 104–5
environment 5–6, 70, 79, 85–94, 99, 102–3, 105–6
epistemology 3, 86, 93
ethnography 87, 93–4, 100, 103, 105–6
Eurasia 94
European Commission 37
European Union (EU) 37
experience of wind 85–109

fansubs 53
farming 86, 92
fascism 55
feelings 18, 57–8, 74, 88, 101
Ferguson, A. 52
fetishization 55, 92
fieldwork 88, 104
fisheries 2–3, 85–109
folklore 86–7, 89, 91–5, 97, 104–6
further research 80
furusato 51, 60, 79, 92
Futenma 5–6, 13–14, 16–20
future generations 20, 92–3

genealogy 90
Geneva Conventions 34
genocide 27–8, 39–40
Germany 1, 34, 39, 41
Ginowan 5, 16–18, 20
globalization 29

habitus theory 92, 103
Hague, The 26–49
haiku 97
Hartley, L.P. 50
Hashimoto, H. 94
hegemony 74, 77, 86, 93
Henoko 5, 13–14
heritage 86, 92, 94, 106
Himawari 93
Himeyuri Peace Museum 6
Hirohito, Emperor 30, 35, 61, 69, 71, 77
Hiroshima 11, 30, 80
Holocaust 33
Honshu 101

Hook, G. 1–25, 80
Hsu, E. 88
Hyakuta, N. 53
hydrogeology 104

Ichikawa 15
identity 2–3, 6–8, 20–2, 29, 38–9; coastal fisheries 86, 103; Kamikazes 55–6, 64, 75, 78, 80; self-identity 51–2, 60–1, 71, 79; war crime tribunals 41–2, 44
ideology 32, 52, 61, 75–6, 78
Iha, Y. 17
imperialism 6, 8, 10–12, 26, 30; Kamikazes 52, 54–5, 57, 60–1, 69–70, 74–8; war crime tribunals 35, 38
Inamine, K. 11–12, 21
India 32
indigenous knowledge (IK) 89
indigenous technical knowledge (ITK) 89
Ingold, T. 10, 86, 90–1
interdisciplinarity 51, 87, 89
international community 1–2, 8, 36–40, 44
International Criminal Court (ICC) 2, 27–9, 33–41, 43–4
international law 30–1, 33–9, 41
International Legal Affairs Bureau 39
International Military Tribunal for the Far East (IMTFE) 2, 9, 27–36, 38–44, 57
interpretation 1, 8, 10–11, 29, 43–4; coastal fisheries 86, 91–5, 101, 104, 106; Kamikazes 51–3, 59, 68, 72–4, 80
invisible landscapes 85–109
Irago Canal 105
Ise Bay 5–7, 11, 13, 15–17, 19–22, 42, 51–2, 87, 95, 99–102, 104
Ishiguro, K. 50
Itoman 10
Iwanami 10
Izu peninsula 103

Japan 1–3; Battle of Okinawa 4–25; coastal fisheries 85–109; Kamikazes 50–84; ministries 8, 35, 38–40; penal code 28, 39–42, 44; tribunals 26–49
Japan Federation of Bar Association (JFBA) 37
Japanese Network for the ICC (JNICC) 37
Jeans, B. 59
jihadism 79
Joel, B. 59

Kadena Air Base 6
Kaifu, T. 14
Kalland, A. 90
Kamikazes 2–3, 50–84
Kamishima-chō 102, 104–5

INDEX

KH Coder 67
Kina, M. 13
Kindai corpus 67
Kishi, N. 31–2
Kokugakuin University 95
Korea 1, 4, 8–9, 27–8, 43–4, 53–5, 57, 60
Kudan 69
Kumanonada Sea 104
kumiaichō 99
Kuzaki-chō 87, 99–104
Kyōto 96
Kyūshū 95

landscapes 2, 80, 85–109
letters 2, 51, 54–62, 69–70, 74–5
Lévi-Strauss, C. 92
lexicography 95
Liberal Democratic Party (LDP) 32, 35–6
licences 101
lobsters 100–1
Low, C. 88
Lukner, K. 2, 9, 26–49
lunar calendar 104

Mabuni 10–11
Manchester United FC 52
manga 52, 56
Marine Corps Air Station Futenma 5–6, 13–14, 16–20
Martinez, D. 99–100
Matsukawa, M. 17
Mecab 67
media 52–4, 56–7, 73, 78
Meiji Period 67, 95
memes 52–3
memorials 7–14, 16, 21, 54–8, 60, 66, 69
memory 1–3; Battle of Okinawa 4–25; coastal fisheries 85–109; collective 2, 6–12, 15, 21, 29, 32, 52, 55–8, 61, 74, 79, 105; contested 1–25, 50–84, 86, 106; Kamikazes 50–84; politics 28–9; recycled 78–80; war crime tribunals 26–49
Memory of the World Register 8, 54
meteorology 86, 88–9, 93–5, 99–100, 102, 104
microclimates 87
Midway, Battle of 63
military 1–2, 4–11, 27, 29–30, 54–5; Battle of Okinawa 13–22; Kamikazes 54–5, 57, 60–1, 69–71, 74, 76, 78; war crime tribunals 34, 36–7
Minami-Kagoshima 54
Ministry of Education, Culture, Sports, Science and Technology (MEXT) 8
Ministry of Foreign Affairs 38–9
Ministry of Justice 35, 40

missives 3, 50–84
Mitsubishi Materials 43
Miyamori School 7, 15–22
Miyazaki, H. 53
modernism 91–2, 106
Mongols 54
monsoons 94–5
Moore, N. 103
Mori, A. 94
Moriyama, M. 35–6
Motoya Bay 103
multidimensional scaling (MDS) 67–8
Murakami, M. 95
museums 1–2, 6–8, 11–12, 17, 21–2, 54–60, 78, 80
Mushanokoji, S. 16

Nagasaki 11, 30, 80
Nago 5
Nakaima, H. 13
Nakayama, M. 92
Nanjing Massacre 55
Nara Institute of Science and Technology 67
narrative 1, 8, 19, 29–30, 32, 43, 56, 73, 80, 102–3
National Institute for Japanese Language and Linguistics 67
nationalism 8–9, 29, 32, 55–7, 61, 76–8
navies 54, 61–3, 69, 74
New Kōmeitō 35–6
Nihon Hōsō Kyōkai (NHK) 53
Nippon Coke and Engineering 43
Nippon Steel 43
Noda, Y. 14
Nomoto, K. 92
Nomura, F. 93, 97, 104
non-governmental organizations (NGOs) 33
non-profit organizations (NPO) 17
North Korea 4
Northeast Asia 42–3
nostalgia 51, 53, 60, 86
nuclear power 4, 80
Nuremberg Tribunal 27, 33–4, 43

Occupation 2, 6, 9, 12, 15–16, 18–19
Ōe, K. 10–11
Okinawa 2, 4–25, 64, 95
Okinawa, Battle of 2, 4–25, 64
Okinawa International University 7, 16–22
Okinawa Law and Politics Research Centre 20
Okinawa Memorial Day 7, 9, 13, 21
Okinawa Memorial Service 12, 14
Ōmi Collection 62, 66, 75
oral history 8, 12, 17, 89, 92–3
orography 99

INDEX

Ōsaka 10, 96
Osaka High Court 10
Ōta, M. 11–12
Oura Bay 5
Owada, S. 34

Pacific Ocean 97, 101, 105
Pacific War 1–2, 8, 10, 55, 77
Pal, R. 30, 32, 39
Pállson, G. 89
peace clause 34
Peace Memorial Park 10
penal code 28, 39–42, 44
People's School Law 77
perception 29, 31–4, 38–9, 42, 70, 85–90, 92, 102–3, 105
perspectives 2–4, 14, 20, 35, 40; coastal fisheries 88, 91–2, 99, 106; Kamikazes 51–2, 54, 78; war crime tribunals 43
Phelan, J. 89
phenomenology 88
Philippines 69
pilots 2, 15, 18, 50–84
place-naming 105
politics 2, 4–5, 7–9, 11–16, 19–22; coastal fisheries 92; Kamikazes 56–8, 60, 64, 66, 73, 80; war crime tribunals 26049
practical knowledge 85, 88–9, 92
Prefectural Peace Museum 7, 11–12, 21
processual knowledge 86, 94
propaganda 56–7, 76, 78
proverbs 101, 103–6
psychology 2, 51, 56, 61, 75

qualitative analysis 2, 61, 64, 67, 72
quantitative analysis 2, 61

Rape of Nanking 1
religion 54, 57–8, 61–2, 64, 66, 69, 100
Resolution 3314 56–7
risk 5–7, 11, 13, 15–17, 19–22, 42, 51–2, 99–100, 104
Rome Statute 34, 36–7, 39–43
Rumsfeld, D. 19
rural areas 89, 93, 105
Russia 57, 77
Russo-Japanese War 77
Ryūkyū 95

Sakima, A. 19
samurai warriors 55
San Francisco Peace Treaty 31, 43
Schnell, S. 94
sea cucumbers 102–3
Sea of Japan 96–7

Sea of Kumano 105
seasonality 85, 87, 93–5, 99–103, 105
Second World War 27–9, 32–3, 38–9, 41, 43–4, 53, 55, 73, 77
sedimented experiences 99–100
Sekiguchi, T. 93, 95–6
self-identity 51–2, 60–1, 71, 79
self-representation 50–84
semiotics 89, 103
Senkaku-Daioyu Islands 54
Seoul High Court 43
September 11 2001 34, 37
Sheeran, E. 59
Shigemitsu, M. 31
Shima Peninsula 99
Shindo, M. 88
Shinohara, T. 92
Shinpū 54, 62
Shintoism 58, 61, 66, 69–71
Showa Period 67
Siberia 95
slavery 8, 26–7, 30, 43–4
social media 52–3, 79
social sciences 94
socio-cognitive representations (SCR) 73
solar calendar 104
Solomon Islands, Battle of 63
songbooks 75–7
South Korea 1, 8–9, 27–8, 43–4, 54
Sovereignty Restoration Day 9
Soviet Union 4
Special Action Committee on Okinawa (SACO) 5, 19
state 1, 7–10, 27–31, 33, 36–9, 42, 55–8, 75–7
Status of Force Agreement 19
Student-Mobilization Law 63
students 6, 18–20, 22, 35, 37, 63, 67, 76
subjectivity 70, 87–9
suicide 10–11, 51–3, 55, 60, 79
Sumitomo Metal 43
symbolism 5, 10, 20, 22, 32, 56–7, 87, 89, 93, 103
Syria 52

Taiwan 69
Tanaka, Y. 60
taxonomy 90, 99–100
terrorism 34, 37, 41
Teruya, N. 14
textbooks 8–9, 26, 75–7
Thought War 77
Toba-shi 104
Tokkō-tai 50–84
Tokyo 2, 9, 16, 26–49

INDEX

Tone River 97
topography 95
tourism 6, 94
Tōyama, K. 35–6
tradition 3, 53, 67, 86–7, 89–95, 101, 104, 106
traditional ecological knowledge (TEK) 89–90
traditional knowledge in local conception (LTK) 91
traditional knowledge in modernist conception (MTK) 91, 106
tribunals 26–49
Trust Fund for Victims (TFV) 43–4
typhoons 99, 101, 103, 105

UNESCO 8, 54–5
unfinished war 4–25
United Kingdom (UK) 1, 69
United Nations (UN) 33, 56–7
United States (US) 2, 4–25, 29–31, 34–5, 37, 54–5, 57, 69
urban areas 94, 105
Uruma 15–16

vernacular tradition 86–7, 94, 103
victimization 2, 5–8, 10–11, 14, 17; Battle of Okinawa 19, 21–2; Kamikaze 54, 56–8; war crime tribunals 28, 30–1, 43
Vietnam War 59

war crime tribunals 26–49
war criminals 2, 9, 26–49, 54, 57
war on terrorism 37, 41
War-Bereaved Families Association 14
weather reports 99–100
West 30, 75
Whealm, Y. 103
winds 3, 53–5, 80, 85–109
World Cup 52
World War II 27–9, 32–3, 38–9, 41, 43–4, 53, 55, 73, 77

Yaeyama 6, 9
Yanagita, K. 92, 94–6
Yasukuni Shrine 1–2, 8–9, 26, 54, 57–8, 64, 69
YouTube 53, 59
Yūshū kan Museum 2, 8, 57–8, 76